Poetry

The Best of 2020

Poets of the World

inner child press international

'building bridges for cultural understanding'

Credits

Poets of the World

Editing

hülya n. yılmaz, Ph. D.

Cover Design

William S. Peters, Sr.
Inner Child Press International

General Information

Poetry ~ The Best of 2020
Poets of the World

1st Edition: 2020

This Publishing is protected under Copyright Law as a "Collection". All rights for all submissions are retained by the individual author and / or artist. No part of this publishing may be reproduced, transferred in any manner without the prior *WRITTEN CONSENT* of the "Material Owner" or its Representative, Inner Child Press. Any such violation infringes upon the Creative and Intellectual Property of the Owner pursuant to International and Federal Copyright Law. Any queries pertaining to this "Collection" should be addressed to Publisher of Record.

Publisher Information:

Inner Child Press
intouch@innerchildpress.com
www.innerchildpress.com

This Collection is protected under U.S. and International Copyright Laws

Copyright © 2020: Inner Child Press

ISBN-13: 978-1-952081-37-8 (inner child press, ltd.)

$ 29.95

*In the darkness of my life
I heard the music
I danced…
and the Light appeared
and I dance*

Janet P. Caldwell

Table of Contents

Preface — xv
A Few Words from the Director of Editing . . . — xvii
Disclaimer — xxi

Poetry ~ The Best of 2020

Mutawaf A. Shaheed	3
Artha Perla	6
Sayeed Abubakar	8
Kavita Ezekiel Mendonca	10
Salaudeen Abdulazeez	13
Eliza Segiet	15
Britney Russell	17
Yuan Changming	19
Andrew Scott	21
Anuradha Bhattacharyya	23
Fernando Jose Martinez Alderete	25
Neelam Saxena Chandra	27
B. S. Tyagi	29
Paul T. Dillon	31
Poul Lynggaard Damgaard	33

Table of Contents... *continued*

John Eliot	36
Kevin M. Hibshman	38
Anna Fletcher	40
Job Degenaar	42
Umid Najjari	44
Ndaba Sibanda	46
Faleeha Hassan	48
Zaldy Carreon De Leon, Jr.	51
Basudhara Roy	56
Zakir Malik	59
Mark Fleisher	61
Tyran Prizren Spahiu	64
Chijioke Ogbuike	66
Dilip Mohapatra	70
June Barefield	73
D' Siafa Draper	76
Monsif Beroual	79
Alicia Minjarez Ramírez	81
Kamrul Islam	83
Langley Shazor	85
Kashiana Singh	87

Table of Contents... continued

Teresa E. Gallion	89
Louise Hudon	91
Suranjit Gain	93
Rajashree Mohapatra	96
Nguyen Chau Ngoc Doan Chinh	98
Attracta Fahy	105
Supratik Sen	107
Zinia Mitra	109
Uwe Friesel	111
Akash Sagar	114
Channah Moshe	116
Armenuhi Sisyan	118
Maria Do Sameiro Barroso	120
Jyoti Nair	122
Galina Italyanskaya	124
Sayak Bhandari	126
Maryam Abbasi	128
Gabriela Nikoloska	130
Mourad Faska	132
Tihomir Jancovski	134
Varsha Das	136

Table of Contents ... *continued*

Joseph S. Spence, Sr.	138
Raed Anis Al-Jishi	140
Iwu Jeff	143
Hannie Rouweler	146
Rubab Abdullah	149
Khalid Imam	152
D. L. Davis	154
Jaydeep Sarangi	157
Eftichia Kapardeli	159
Nigar Arif	162
Miled Khaldi	165
Linda Imbler	168
Babatunde Waliyullah Adesokan	170
Lucky Stephen Onyah	173
Padmaja Iyengar-Paddy	175
Rini Valentina	177
Ashok K. Bhargava	179
Christena AV Williams	181
Kay Salady	184
Thirupurasundari CJ	186
Ratan Ghosh	189

Table of Contents... *continued*

Warda Zerguine	191
Hassan Hegazy Hassan	193
Iram Fatima 'Ashi'	196
Eden Soriano Trinidad	198
Yvette Murrell	200
Semih Bilgiç	202
Somasuntharampillai Pathmanathan	204
Laura Fitzgerald	208
Nket-Awaji Alpheaus	212
Nataša Sardžoska	215
Brindha Vinodh	217
Ishfaq SaAhil	219
Terri L. Johnson	222
Molly Joseph	225
Ifeanyi John Nwokeabia	228
Eduard Harents	230
John Chizoba Vincent	232
Asoke Kumar Mitra	235
Alonzo Gross	238
Pragya Sharma	241
Ashok Chakravarthy Tholana	243

Table of Contents... *continued*

Ramesh Reddy Tera	245
Hussein Habasch	247
Meera Rao	252
Marcelo Sánchez	254
Gino Leineweber	257
C. S. P. Shrivastava	259
Ramón de Jesús Núñez Duval	261
Nosakhare Collins	263
Surekha Anandraya Bhat	265
Ranjana Sharan Sinha	267
Ro Hamedullah	270
Craig Alton Kirkland	272
Elizabeth Kurian 'Mona'	274
Finlay Hall	276
Shareef Abdur-Rasheed	279
Ananda Nepali	283
Tarana Turan Rahimli	285
Laure Charazac	287
Ann Christine Tabaka	289
David Winship	291
Ibaa Ismail	293

Table of Contents ... *continued*

Shakil Kalam	297
Ibrahim Honjo	299
Annie Pothen	302
Aneek Chatterjee	304
Vandana Kumar	306
Rehanul Hoque	309
Rosy Lidia Alosious	312
Tapas Dey	314
Alicja Maria Kuberska	316
Gobinda Biswas	318
Ajanta Paul	320
Nandita De nee Chatterjee	322
Vidya Shankar	327
Robert Gibbons	330
Tangirala Sree Latha	333
Padmini Janardhanan	335
Elvirawati Pasila	337
Marilyn Thomas King	339
Rofiat Omobolanle Kareem	341
Divya Sinha	343
Helen Campbell	345

Table of Contents... continued

Lovelyn P. Eyo	347
Oyewole Barakat Tobiloba	350
Julius Joy Oluwaseun	352
Mircea Dan Duta	355
Priyanka Tiwari	362
Colombe Mimi Leland	365
Glenn Johnson	367
Ayo Ayoola-Amale	373
Smrutiranjan Mohanty	375
Basab Mondal	378
Seena Sreevalson	380
Padmapriya Karthik	382
Madhumathi H.	384
Orbindu Ganga	388
Anwesha Paul	392
Annapurna Sharma A.	394
Queen Sarkar	396
Adesunwon Babatunde Habideen	398
Zana Coven	400
Tejaswini Patil	403
Bozena Helena Mazur-Nowak	405

Table of Contents ... *continued*

Jyotirmaya Thakur	407
Ashok Kumar	409
Olaifa Omodolapo Roseline	411
Mahmoud Said Kawash	414
Keisha Ballentyne	417
NRK Srikar	419
Shoma Bhowmick	421
Abhilipsa Kuanar	423
Shiv Raj Pradhan	426
Michelle Joan Barulich	428
D. L. Lang	431
Hema Ravi	433
hülya n. yılmaz	435
William S. Peters, Sr.	440

Epilogue 443

About Inner Child Press International	445
ICPI Board of Directors	447
ICPI Cultural Ambassadors	448
Other Socially Important Anthologies	449

Poets, Writers . . . know that we are the enchanting magicians that nourish the seeds of dreams and thoughts . . . it is our words that entice the hearts and minds of others to believe there is something grand about the possibilities that life has to offer and our words tease it forth into action . . . for you are the Poet, the Writer to whom the Gift of Words has been entrusted . . .

William S. Peters, Sr.

Preface

At Inner Child Press International, we are always seeking a means to provoke the poets and writers of our world to share their oft unique perspectives, be it conscious, sub-conscious or otherwise. We do this through anthologies, a coming together of the diverse cultures from around the world. Many times in reading, you can detect some cultural nuances that offer insight. For the most part, what is achieved in these themed anthological collections of poetry and prose we publish, is a sort of human congruity, a confluence of voices that provides each of us a clear and succinct understanding, that we humans, wherever we hail from, are more alike, more similar than we are dissimilar.

Though we publish quite a number of individual author's volumes as well, which I thoroughly enjoy; anthologies hold a unique position in my spiritual assignment. The opportunity to witness our own microcosmic pilgrimage to the making of an anthology is a true and honorable marvel to take part in.

In the following pages, be blessed, and take a few moments of your time to read and consider our commonality as well as our differences culturally and that of perspective. ENJOY!

Visit our web site and our "Anthologies" section for more publications available for purchase and FREE Downloads.

Thank you
Bless Up

William S. Peters, Sr.
Poet, Writer, Activist, Publisher
Inner Child Press International

'building bridges of cultural understanding'

*Poets . . .
sowing seeds in the
Conscious Garden of Life,
that those who have yet to come
may enjoy the Flowers.*

A Few Words from the Director of Editing...

Poetry ~ The Best of 2020 marks itself as the last anthology that Inner Child Press International is offering for the year 2020. This publication follows a strong line of volumes which include *Corona . . . Social Distancing*, *World Healing World Peace 2020*, *The Heart of a Poet* and *W. A. R. ~ We Are Revolution*. In the ICPI-tradition, an invitation was also extended to writers from across the globe to be considered as contributors for this collective project. Once again, hundreds have embraced the idea of yet another gathering of diverse linguistic, professional, personal backgrounds and experiences on a platform of perhaps the most-overlooked and underappreciated literary genre: poetry. Our call was simple: "Send us your one best poem." The response was overwhelmingly generous and enthusiastic as an exceptional choir of creative voices celebrated our invite with a warm embrace. Thus, the current display of a worldwide aspiration for unity in diversity has transpired.

As has been the case with our previous anthological collaborations, a look at the languages that our participating writers represent in this collection suffices to note the vast richness of resourceful expressions: Hindi, Arabic, Bosnian, French, Polish, Italian, Nepali, Armenian, Czech, Spanish, Russian, Turkish, Burmese, German, Indonesian, Swedish, Hebrew, Macedonian, Kurdish, Danish, Dutch, Indonesian, Albanian, Filipino, Hungarian, Irish, Greek, Azerbaijani, Bengali, Portuguese, Chewa, Serbian, Irish Gaelic, Scottish Gaelic, Urdu, and Vietnamese. Though in only a few cases, poems in native tongues precede their English translations, giving us all a uniquely intimate glimpse into at least the external appearance of the creative writing process. The overall product of beauty has been, once again, the joining of hands by a multitude of authentic sources from the core of their cultures; thus, 'building bridges of cultural understanding'.

I know what is expected of me at this point; namely, in specific reference to providing an insight into the discipline of editing. Instead of reinventing the wheel, I will simply echo some of my comments that I have shared with our readership in our previous anthological work. The process of implementing editorial steps within the context of an international volume does, after all, not differ substantially when the integral promise of Inner Child Press International is taken into consideration: to preserve the original entries in our attempts to maintain the integrity of the poets' voices in order for the reader to enjoy each poem's authenticity. What I state in our disclaimer on behalf of our Department of Editing Services cannot be stressed enough: as we have elected to do minimal surface editing with minor adjustments, you may encounter some challenges in achieving total clarity of the messages shared through poetry. Regardless! I will indulge you to let go of your critical thinking and embrace the spirit through words offered for the poetic art. Having stated thus, I still would like to add a few words about the particulars of our editorial work for our anthologies.

Compilations of a large body of work of any literary genre present a variety of formalistic and artistic challenges, even in situations when all writings originate from a single language. The difficulty of the task at hand increases proportionately as more languages form the basis of the writings that are collected. Contextual challenges often reside in the texts of non-native English speakers or in their translations of those texts into English. Some may (and do) argue that all such submissions should be edited thoroughly before they are offered to the public. It is exactly at this point where I want to stress my professional insight with utmost emphasis: editing is not the exact science one would expect. Many times, when an editor considers and employs the rules of English upon a translated work or upon one that might not have been composed in English first, the authenticity of the authors' words and meaning face the risk of being subjected to a misrepresentation. Writings with a dialectal, colloquial or eclectic style are exposed to the same risk when the scrutiny of editing is concerned. Too often, the resulting loss of the authorial voice can be profound and deprive the reader of the genuine aspects of the writers' thoughts, feelings and innate flavor. At Inner Child Press International, we strive to maintain the integrity of each and every author's offerings by preserving the seemingly-awkward expressions of those whose native language is not of our own.

Our invitation to the reader remains the same as within all of our anthological offerings: to take time to indulge each contributor for her / his own creativity and aspirations to convey her / his uniqueness.

hülya n. yılmaz, Ph.D.
Professor Emerita, The Pennsylvania State University
Director of Editing Services, Inner Child Press International

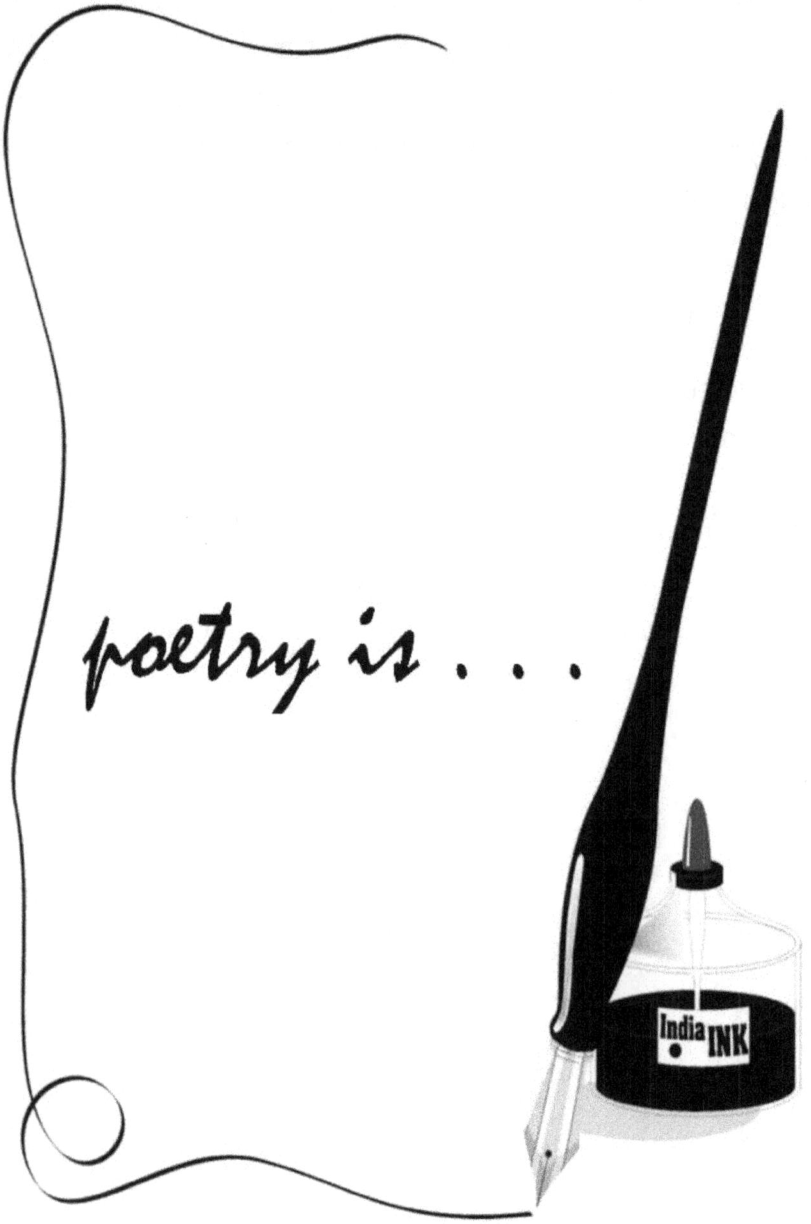

poetry is . . .

Disclaimer

In our attempts to maintain the integrity of the poets' voices in the publication before you, *Poetry ~ The Best of 2020*, we have elected to do minimal surface editing. We felt that preserving the original entries was critically important for you, the reader, to enjoy each poem's authenticity.

All poems have been preserved in their original versions. You may encounter a few challenges in achieving total clarity of the messages shared through poetry, but I indulge you to let go of your critical thinking and embrace the spirit through words offered for the poetic art.

From the desk of . . .

hülya n. yılmaz, Ph.D.
Director of Editing

Inner Child Press International
'building bridges of cultural understanding'

WHAT WOULD LIFE BE WITHOUT A LITTLE POETRY?

Poetry

The Best of 2020

Poets of the World

Poets of the World

Poetry... The Best of 2020

Mutawaf A. Shaheed, AKA C. E. Shy, has been writing since the seventh grade throughout high school, until he became more involved in sports. After his graduation, this widely published author worked at White Motors Company. "The Poet's Corner", his column in the company's newspaper, constitutes his first publication.

www.facebook.com/mutawaf.shaheed

Impressions
Mutawaf A. Shaheed, AKA C. E. Shy

Opening my windows thinking that
I may get the rest of the fresh
air that was left there just two
minutes ago. Then the wind said,
"not really."

With cinnamon coffee in tow, I continue
to work on the suggestions, of the could
haves. The what ifs, didn't fit. Squelching
the possibilities of being younger as
tomorrow glides by, today, shaking its head
and saying, "I don't think so."

Drawing thin lines between passion and
Romance, taking a chance that they may
be the same. You think so? It may be
easier to take the blame, than to try and
explain, why or why not.

In the process of maintaining bits of sanity,
I believe I go completely mad in the process
of elimination. People find themselves in a
strain attempting to understand why they,
can't be them.

Semi-finally, they find devices that bring
them to the brink of temporary. Libraries
filled with agony. Bookshelves lined with
mis-directions. Finding relief from grief in
whiskey and soda.

Evolution gone wrong, singing songs backwards
to come up with something that can't possibly
add up. No more benefits in one and one making
two. Waiting to hear the gun shots after the shout,
these are the sounds one can hear while hoping
they aren't next.

Pinning their hopes on Bar Be Que ribs, just as grandma did,
thinking that somebody is coming back to
endorse them, makes for the completion of the final
act of act one. A tragedy at best.

Artha Perla, research assistant in the Department of English (Mangalore University, Karnataka), writes art reviews for regional newspapers and magazines. She has *Nanna Putta Tamma*, a poem collection in Kannada, to her credit. As a Bharatanatyam dancer and student of Carnatic Classical music, she personally contributes to art and culture.

Hope
Artha Perla

Everyday I'm looking for hope –

Turning to my side to see him sleep,
Peaceful countenance snoozing hardships quite.

Everyday I'm looking for hope –

Sliding the door to the sounds of the world,
Letting the living soak in the bright.

Everyday I'm looking for hope –

Fluttering flies eager for its mate,
Jogs me of his loving gaze –

Everyday I'm looking for hope –

In the whistling cooker, boiling milk,
In the smiles around and in those eyes –

Everyday I'm looking for hope -

Unsettling ants, scurrying squirrels,
Drizzling rain, sprouting grain,
Hop of the birds and the cock-a-doodle-do,
All prevent me refrain!

Born on September 21, 1972 in Bangladesh, Sayeed Abubakar writes modern epic poetry in Bengali. He has more than 25 books to his credit. His famous two collections are *Mujibnama* (2018) and *Nabinama* (2020). He has been recognized as one of the top 500 poets in Poemhunter.com.

I Am Tired of Seeing
Sayeed Abubakar

I am tired of seeing the beautiful earth
Getting damaged by those beasts who look like
Men too. All the thrones have been occupied
By those everywhere who have no souls, no

Love, no sympathy to men; they only
Reign with harshness and hatred; they don't care
Justice, morality, rationality;
Greed, lust, brutality are their weapons.

I am tired of seeing genocide after
Genocide on this beautiful earth where
Men, women and children are crying and dying,
Where killers are the heroes, where evils

Are considered good, fools are honored and
The communal and the capitalist
Show their sharp teeth as if they were hungry
Sharks, hyenas, tigers or crocodiles.

Poets of the World

Kavita Ezekiel Mendonca, born to and raised in a Jewish family in Mumbai, went to Mumbai's Queen Mary School. She has a B.A. in English and French, an M.A. from the University of Bombay in English and American Literature, and a Master's Degree in Education from Oxford Brookes University, England.

Mother
Kavita Ezekiel Mendonca

Mother had three sarees
Two were 'inside sarees' to wear in the house
The third was the 'going out' saree to wear for occasions,
She could wear the 'inside' one to the bazaar
Which was outside the house,
So that was the "inside-outside" saree.

Mother fried onions at four-thirty in the morning.
When they became too expensive, we rejoiced
She made the curry without onions,
Then there was no smell and our sleep was blissful.
At five-thirty she packed 'hot lunch'
Into lunch boxes.
With no microwaves we ate our 'hot lunch' cold,
With few ingredients and a limited budget
Mother's food was heavenly.
She took cooking lessons from Premila Lal.

In mother's world you had to eat the egg soft-boiled
Or egg-flip, if you had sports practice
At six-thirty in the morning,
Egg-flip was raw egg in warm milk
No nutmeg. Condiments are expensive
Only for the rich.
Close your nose and drink it up, or down.
If you didn't, she would hold your nose
For you and you couldn't breathe.

Mother had an idiom for everything,
Some she recited in English, others in Marathi
If you failed a math test, it was
'Don't cry over spilt milk,'
She said my daddy was 'too clever by half'* (sounded better in Marathi)
If he rationalized matters by 'clever' intellectual arguments,
Remember he was a poet!

Poets of the World

One day she took me to see the Principal of her old school
Who asked how my daddy was
My reply, 'my daddy is too clever by half.'
Mother did not flinch when the Principal asked
Where I had learned that expression.

Mother rolled her eyes to communicate commands
She rolled one lip over the other, pressing them hard together
It was a language learned in childhood
A call to prompt response as children.

Once I tried to express disapproval of a student's behaviour
I rolled my eyes and pressed my lips together hard
He burst out laughing, I failed to understand his response
Mother's face appeared before me
More practice might be needed.

Many things in the world according to my mother
Make so much sense to me now.
The ritual of hand-washing, great for Pandemic times,
Between fingers, in, out, over palms under hands
Her legacy of 'Waste not, Want not'
And 'Saving for a Rainy Day'
And her prophecy for my future
"The world will become a more difficult place for you
And even more difficult for your children
But remember that God is great."
I'm glad I inherited her faith.

*'Too clever by half' in idiomatic usage refers to being too clever for your own good.

Salaudeen Abdulazeez, with his pen name "Hayzedbaba", is a poet, a student and an author. He has won several awards for his poems, such as "The Best Poet" prize from The Writers Pen and a Blue Quill from Poemarium.

Homelessness
Salaudeen Abdulazeez, AKA Hayzedbaba

It unbearable when it cold.
The cold will penetrate my bones.
Every heads will be in their respective abode to shell a burning flame.
When I have nowhere to shell my own flame.
When it sunny days my body burn like firewood.
Absence of intermediary between sun and me.
Passers-by watching me in my dirty clothe sleeping along the road,
The cloud is my roof, the floor is bed.
Anyone who come in contact with someone like me try to help.
The situation here is unfavorable.
I feel pain from my head to my humble toes.
The taste of all weather conditions I have tasted.
Rain beat me like cane.
Where is my own home?
When will I be at my own protective roof?
The pain is becoming a monster.
It wakes me when am sleeping.
It keeps me awake when I feel like sleeping.

Eliza Segiet has a Master's Degree in Philosophy (Jagiellonian University). Her poem, "Questions and Sea of Mists", won the International Publication of the Year title from Spillwords Press (2017 and 2018). She was nominated for the 2019 Pushcart Prize, the iWoman Global Awards, and the 2020 Laureate Naji Naaman Literary Prize.

Life's Plan
Eliza Segiet

Is this what autumn looks like?
Through deserted streets,
in spouts of rain,
unhurried
the eve strolls around.

Very slowly
gives time to a long
granting time for talks
night
about how it can be.

Regular
- life plan,
which is worth
a look
- even
through water pour windows.

When the rain stops,
dreams have a chance
to stop being themselves.

This is what autumn looks like
- now plans won't be misty.

Translated by Ula de B

Britney Russell, a 23-year-old poet from Jamaica, has been on multiple radio stations and poetry shows in the USA, Canada, South Africa, and the United Kingdom. Poetry has perpetually been one with her since childhood. She was placed second in the Pledge Nexus International Poetry competition on September 1, 2020.

Blackness Is Royalty
Britney Russell

The sun kissed my skin,
Thank God for my beautiful melanin.
Whether chestnut, almond or chocolate
Black girls are winning.

The water hugged my hair,
It appreciated the kinky flair.
My natural hair, I will perpetually wear.

It identifies who we are, whether far or near.
They planted the seed that we were always slaves.
But we were kings, queens and they were afraid:
Afraid of how powerful we were and are.
They raped Africa and left a monumental scar.

Let's take back our culture and throne!
Appreciate and love our blackness to the bone.
Rise up and discover the truth!
All along we've been lied to about our roots.

Yuan Changming edits *Poetry Pacific* with Allen Yuan in Vancouver. Credits include ten Pushcart nominations, six poetry awards as well as publications in *Best of the Best Canadian Poetry (2008-17), & BestNewPoemsOnline,* among others across 46 countries.

For the Other Side of the Night: A Sinnet Sonnet
Yuan Changming

Since	yester twilight
Along	the borderline of tonight
With	fits of thirst & hunger
Among	storms of pain
Under	attacks of viruses
Between	interludes of insomnia
Beyond	both hope & expectation

At	the depth of darkness
Amidst	the nightmare
Through	one tiny antlike moment
After	another…
Against	deadly despair
Until	awakening
To	the first ray of dawn

Andrew Scott is a native of Fredericton, NB, Canada. During his time as a poet, he has spoken in front of classrooms, judged poetry competitions, and authored over 200 hundred publications. Scott has six collections of poems and one book of photography to his credit.

The Sky Is Angry
Andrew Scott

The sky is screaming angry.
The winds are swirling blindly
in the dark with a purpose.

Spirits are looking over the world
from just over the edge.
Bodies are afraid to step over.
Chaos voices holding back all.

Standing in the middle of the storm
I am pretending to be full of strength
even though people's screams of pain
are making myself so weak.

Humans have stopped being civil.
Killing each other from a slight.
Peace is not on the horizon.
Fires are still burning,
Spreading from person to person.

Voices of peace not being heard.
Civility has been extinguished.
Concern that sensibility
will never come back.

Enough has become enough.
The sky is clashing angrily
and my soul is afraid.

Dr. Anuradha Bhattacharyya, Associate Professor of English in a government college in Chandigarh, India, has authored four poetry books, three novels, and two academic books. She won 5 prestigious awards in the field of literature. She was one of the four jury members in the Lit Digital Awards 2020, India.

Cerebration
Anuradha Bhattacharyya

Bread and cheese for brunch,
A drumstick for dinner, light, evenly roasted,
Intake for the day.
One way to expel CO_2 is cycling to the lake . . .
Yet clammy skin stinks
And I am not going to let it.

More poised am I with a laptop
A reclining floor sofa for gaming,
A mug full of green tea
With raisins
That's right.

Inertia in the bones
For blood to work on synapses
Click click
Go the keys.

Dry skin, dry lips,
Dry eyed
Concentration.

Dedication
Towards a single goal.

Perfect.

Poetry... The Best of 2020

Born in Leon Guanajuato Mexico on April 21, 1977, Fernando Martinez Alderete is a writer, poet, theater actor, and radio producer. His poems appeared in 108 anthologies in thirteen countries around the world. He has authored two books, one of poetry and another of short stories.

Radiography
Fernando Jose Martinez Alderete

I am not a man of total steel,
Many people in society sanctify me
for being in a wheelchair desensitized
like a trunk that only breathes casually.

There is a weakness in the interior that drives me crazy
for the woman and her fragile intrinsic seduction,
I believe I am a knight of inexorable respect
without silencing my delight for muses, although married.

I do not avoid eroticism if it is delicately shown,
nor to the temptation of revenge when they invade
those who imagine that because I am gentle I am helpless,
forgiveness prevails, but what is learned remains.

I will never be steel because I am limited in movements,
If you do me a deep X-ray, you will see my hell,
a mysterious sweetness capable of overflowing bones
when the rhythmic syncopation of an idyllic is ensued.

I'm glad that I was born human but I do not walk,
lover of meat, pasta, cheeses, fruits and chocolates,
flying over any stone or mountain that crosses.

Neelam Saxena Chandra has authored 57 books. She holds a 2015-record with the Limca Book of Records for being the author having the highest number of publications. She has won several international and national awards and was listed in *Forbes* as one of the popular authors in 2014.

A Tearful Adieu
Neelam Saxena Chandra

Mom, so secured was I in your womb;
My life inside you was a real miracle!
My tiny feet swam in glee;
My little hands cuddled you merrily;
My toothless mouth would often giggle and cackle!

Mom, so happy was I in your womb;
But, one day, some quivering clatters I could hear -
I heard someone scream and roar,
"I don't want daughters anymore!"
I sobbed as I listened to your helpless tears . . .

Mom, how could I smile in your womb
When I had understood that being a daughter was so bad?
My little eyes cried and heart yelled;
Something in me had already failed,
Alas, I realized that I would soon be dead!

Mom, although I shall no longer dwell in your womb,
Your warmth and affection I shall surely miss . . .
To you, I shall not lie;
I had not expected to die:
But fate had in store for me this deathly kiss!

Mom, so happy I am to have been a part of your womb,
Although the togetherness was destined as a short boon!
As death pounces and approaches near,
I bid you a tearful adieu mom dear,
May a hundred sons be born to you soon!

Hailing from India, B. S. Tyagi writes in Hindi and English. He has authored several fiction and non-fiction books and translated numerous poetry books. His poems and short stories appeared in various anthologies. He finds the greatest reward in the inner bliss that creativity showered upon him, and not in public recognitions and celebrations.

Celebration
B. S. Tyagi

(1)

The beach splashed with morning hues
Serene and sequestered like a rain-bow
Standing in complete awe I see
A silver wave come towards me
In a jiffy I was inundated
And stayed no more
What I was a moment before.

(2)

Buried I lay under the seas
Delicious coolness I felt seep in
Every pore lay parched for long
Ecstasy spilled all over
Soul fluttered as if in breeze
Strange to say
Thirst – ages long was quenched.

(3)

A song sans words out of bliss issued
Thrilling the whole being
With ecstatic realization
Of Immortality latent within
Utterly spaced out
Deep down I went and went
Here began the Celebration!

Paul T. Dillon has authored three poetry collections (published by Lapwing Publications in Belfast, Northern Ireland). The titles are, *Going Home*, *The Ironmonger's Wolf* and *Invisible Light*. His poems have appeared in magazines and journals in Ireland, the UK and the USA. He lives in Co. Wicklow, Ireland.

The Sea Shell-Child
Paul T. Dillon

And there will be sea shells
For you to gather in the hem
Of your dress for spilling out
Like treasures fashioned into mystery
By the breathing of the sea

Poul Lynggaard Damgaard, a Danish poet, born on the 24th of December, 1977, lives in Aarhus, Denmark. A member of the Danish Authors' Society, he has participated in several international poetry festivals in Europe. His poems have been translated into many different languages.

Vi ville
Poul Lynggaard Damgaard

Vi ville have en anden duft end rosens.
En der forbandt bilerne dybere
end mellem torne
og kronblade.
En feber
mere blank
end kontinentet
som en frossen sø
ingen vil skøjte på.
Hinanden
i et forsinket
bryllupsoptog
på kanten af en farve.
Vi ville hosten som en provokation.

We Wanted
Poul Lynggaard Damgaard

We wanted something else than the scent of roses.
Something that connected the cars deeper
than between thorns
and petals.
A fever
brighter
than the continent.
A frozen lake
no one wants to skate on.
Each other
in a delayed
wedding procession
on the edge of a color.
We wanted the cough as a provocation.

Poets of the World

John Eliot's poetry has been published by Mosaique Press. His works include *Ssh* (2014), *Don't Go* (2016), *Turn on the Dark* (2018), and *Canzoni Del Vernerdi Sera* (2020). His newest collection, a translation of selected poems into Italian, was launched at the Salerno festival in Italy this year.

Messenger

John Eliot
For Daria, March 2020

4.10 a.m. I'm not looking for someone awake,
just saw you on line, don't really know you. We met,
I found you cold. My wife tells me you are warm, kind;
maybe it was me, full of himself, *il poeta,*
the concert. Signed a lot of books that night in
late sun and beauty of small Italian town.
Now you, me, are both awake, afraid of the unknown.
Guns and terrorist belong somewhere else;
soldiers defend us, us against them.
But this. We lie separate in our beds in the dark, waiting.
The air we breathe may be deadly.
For me. For you. For those we love.
There is no reply. Are you the next victim?

Poets of the World

Kevin M. Hibshman has had his poetry, reviews and collages published around the world, most recently in *Rye Whiskey Review*, *The Crossroads*, *Drinkers Only*, *1870*, *Synchronized Chaos*, and *Medusa's Kitchen*.

Love Is the Thread of Our Lives
Kevin M. Hibshman

Each of us a patch of mottled fabric.
Let us weave a tapestry of bold design.
All of our many colors sitting next to each other like
The rainbow in our Creator's eyes.

Love is the thread that truly binds.
There can be no borders if we are to be free.
Each square is self-defined, vibrant in its individuality.

If there are those who feel that they do not belong,
Let us show them just where they fit.
Here we exist neighbor to neighbor, brothers and sisters, stitch to stitch.

One day, when the quilt has been completed,
We will throw it over the cold shoulders of the world.
We will then realize how every color was needed.
Our single flag shall be unfurled.

Poets of the World

Anna Fletcher is a poet, writer, and playwright from Plymouth, the UK. Several of her poems have appeared in numerous national and global anthologies. She is currently working on her own collection for publication. She also writes articles on various topics, including poetry and mental health.

anna.fletcher79@hotmail.co.uk

Inside a Dream
Anna Fletcher

Behind the quietest part of the night
As lucid lullabies drift from the moon,
Since slumber trickles towards dawn's new light;
Stars fading away while covers lay strewn.
Rhythmical rises and falls of the chest,
Deep and heavy, like an elephant's sigh,
Undisturbed dormancy awaits the crest
For waking life to ignite in the eye . . .
Cool cornflower skies, long lavender field,
White waterfalls meandering to space,
Sparkles of stardust; dimensions concealed
Morpheus appears, revealing your face.
Apollo follows, destroying the scene
Exiled and awake, and outside the dream.

Job Degenaar, born in 1952 in The Netherlands, has authored more than a dozen collections of poems. He translated poetry from Paul McCartney, Reiner Kunze and persecuted writers into Dutch. He is the president of PEN Emergency Fund, a worldwide operating fund for writers who urgently need help.

www.jobdegenaar.nl
www.penemergencyfund.com

Hummingbirds Forever
Job Degenaar

(*Inspired by Felicidade, Bernadete Claudino, 2017*)

So smooth the childhood hills, with fields
full of sunflowers, shining in a dancing light

where the hummingbirds have now returned, passing by
like ancient drones, forward, backward, high, low

Purifying nectar with raging wings, deep
from sweet chalices, they hang still

in the moment, writing slow
rules about happiness, sublime

circling around ultimate pleasure
as disciples for their worshiped god

You always wanted to accompany them
and freeze their flight on canvas

just before they disappear, over the Brazilian
hills, behind the wordless mountains

Umid Najjari was born in 15 April, 1989 in Tabriz-Sout, Azerbaijan (Iran). *The Land of the Birds*, *The Photo of the Darkness* and *Beyond the Walls* are among his published writings in addition to some translations.

The Shadow of Longing
Umid Najjari

The shadow of longing enters us, when we don't wait
The cloud of loneliness crosses overhead
The months pass . . .
Our years miss for spring
Our prays loss God

. . . The light of our dream-built house faints
In one moment we are turned to night
Lonely alley in one moment . . .!

. . . Loneliness is not a movie for watching,
The captain of drown ship knows the loneliness,
Not actor knows crying.
Sometimes laughing is the last breath of crying
For that
I laugh for you leaving when I watch your photo.

. . . Ask the standing wall my fatigue
Ask my longing watch . . .!

. . . Miss instead of me,
Miss for feet-seized trees,
Miss for wingless birds like me,
Miss for loneliness,
Miss . . .!

Ndaba Sibanda is the author of *Notes, Themes, Things And Other Things*, *The Gushungo Way*, *Sleeping Rivers*, *Love O'clock*, *The Dead Must Be Sobbing*, *Football of Fools*, *Cutting-edge Cache*, *Of the Saliva and the Tongue*, *When Inspiration Sings In Silence*, *The Way Forward*, *The Ndaba Jamela*, and *Collections and Poetry Pharmacy*.

The Magic of the Rainbow
Ndaba Sibanda

There is something intriguing
about a rainbow of nationalities
and a kaleidoscope of ethnicities
not only about their various cultures,
their colours, creeds and languages,
their interests, hobbies and visions
their farming, fooling, food and music,
but also about their understanding
of the sense of humanity and history
rooted in their many traditional stories,
imbedded and loud in their ethnic clothing,
their lives rich in colour, diversity & detail,
teaching us about our diverse walks in life
and the need to embrace the human race
in its diversity and depth as it is both a unit
and a badge of beauty, ability and creativity

Faleeha Hassan, a writer, teacher, playwright and an editor from Iraq, lives in the U.S.A. She has an M.A. in Arabic literature, authored 25 books, and is the first Iraqi woman who wrote poetry for children. ICPI's Cultural Ambassador for Iraq and the U.S.A. and a 2018 Pulitzer Prize nominee, Hassan's poems have been translated into 16 different languages.

About War, I'm Talking
Faleeha Hassan

What if I slept all that time
Or
I had hibernated from 1980 to 1988?
To be a safe bear
Or wood frog with full body parts
Is much better than being locked in a damaged soul
Your meaning of existence is peeling harshly
Whenever the storm of war is blowing,
Yes,
I remember
In the time of war
The soldiers' mothers
Are unable to pass their hands through the thickness of the walls of absence,
To gently smooth the hair of their boys
Or wipe their dusty faces,
Time after time
Disappointment hits them non-stop
like a squash ball in the hand of a beginner player
While hope keeps escaping from their hearts as nimble as a cat
In the end
They will not cry
But their eyes are melting
Drop by drop
Now
Invisibles like us,
They wish they could heal
From the brain perforating
Siren
And not wake up
Everyday
Shouting in the ears of the house
I am here

I am here
Like someone reading a unmemorized manuscript
invisibles like us
Afraid
One day the lips of the bombs
Will drown them with hot kisses
. . .
1980 to 1988 , the duration of the Iran–Iraq War
wood frog, this frog dies in the winter time and comes back to life in summer

Zaldy Carreon De Leon, Jr. holds a degree in Theology (Magna Cum Laude) and Religious Education (Bene Meritus), and has earned a Doctor Honoris Causa in Literature and Arts (Litt.D.) and Peace and Humanities (DHum). He is a scholar, published author and a licensed teacher at Bataan (The Philippines).

Something About Ilion
Zaldy Carreon De Leon, Jr.

O immortal one, anger's still unsung,
Doomed and ruinous, Akhilleus' fang,
Causing the Akhaians a bitter loss,
Heaving souls their fall, down their brave heroes!
Lo, their flesh upon depressed soil of tears,
In the under-gloom of death disappears,
Leaving but memorials of death and blood,
Carrion for birds of prey and dogs in mud.

Let the will of Zeus be done, this time on,
Whilst heaven attests to the future throne.
When two brave souls contended against,
Broke each other's name their powerful raze,
Lord Agamemnon, Marshall of the Greeks,
And most arduous fright, called prince of the beasts.
The former, Atreus' son, lord and king,
The latter, Akhilleus, goddess bring!

To the gods of Olympus, I beseech,
Who brought this quarrel in a height bewitched?
That peace may not settle that easily,
But a brawl in which our contenders see.
Thus, the son of Zeus by Leto bespeak,
His anger unto Agamemnon's wick,
This man so rude his words and iron will,
To a god nonetheless might keep him still.

Therefore, the god made a great burning wind,
To consume the army, lessen it thin,
So the plague arise, and the army woed,
Sickened and dying in the whole abode,
The curse named for a single man has been

The army's plead to surrender his din,
From despising a man of prayer, flee,
Look how suffer they, this calamity?

This old priest, the man of prayer, Khryses,
In a ship comes down with gifts so priceless,
A mean to ransom his fair daughter back,
This he pursue to Agamemnon's mock,
Thus, on a golden staff he carried on,
The white bands of god, more than precious stone,
He plead for grace to all men Akhaian,
Chiefly to the two powers in the land!

Says Khryses, "O captains, honor I say,
Thou Menelaos, brother-master, pray,
And Agamemnon mighty-king, and all
Thou, Akhaian men, listen to my soul!
Olympus beholds the gods in that grace,
May they grant you plunder to Priam's place,
And that afterwards, a fair wind to home,
But give back my daughter for a ransom."

Then, all the soldiers murmured their assent:
"O Menelaos, Agamemnon, spend
No time to think of this good man's request,
As we too honored Apollo, arrow's best!
Thus, behave well to the priest, O great king,
Take the ransom, give his daughter you bring,
For see how this priest's blessing for us may,
In Priam's gallantry we shall but stay!"

But Agamemnon's rash would not comply,
It went against his desire, so he deny,
And brutally ordered the old priest out,
To the eyes of the gods such act's uncouth,
Says Agamemnon, "Let me not find you,

Poets of the World

Anywhere by the waters or land, sue
Me unto your gods, but I won't comply,
I am Agamemnon, and you know why . . .

Return not, you old priest, never come back,
Forget your daughter in my hands a-luck,
And if I do, those effects can't help you,
The white bands of your gods will say adieu,
They will fail your heart until you die soon,
And see nay your daughter thus if you swoon,
Should I give her up? No, I will not do,
But she's mine forever, I swear to you.

She will grow old at my home in Argos,
Far away from her own country, or worse,
Works on my loom, and visiting my bed,
This shall be her fate as my will has said.
So leave us in peace and go, while you can,
Do not show your face again to me! Ran
Away! – if ever you found my shadow,
Do not come back and witness your sorrow."

So harsh he was, in a voice of terror,
The priest's knees shook, he gets out of the door,
That the old man feared, thus obeyed his word,
Moves away silently, dread by the lord.
But unto the shore, a clamorous sea,
He prayed and prayed to the gods, intensely,
As he cease from solemn, as he forego,
Silken-braided god, summons for Leto:

"O hear me, master of the silver bow,
Righteous protector of Tenedos, know
That your servant here pleads, render my woe!
Your holy towns summon you, Apollo!
O Sminthian, I have been loyal vast,

Roofed your temples and shrines, as do I must,
Golden cups and silver bowls in your name,
Bronze statues and iron swords, just the same.

Or burnt thighbones and fat in your altar,
These things I've done for your glory stellar!
For highly we venerate your strength wide,
Hear your humble servant, my soul unhide,
Bullock or goat flesh – let my wish come true,
An old man's heart has just one thing for you,
But your arrows on the Danaäns strike,
Recompense my tears, snare the way you like."

Basudhara Roy teaches English at Karim City College in Jamshedpur (Jharkhand, India). As an academic, a poet and a reviewer, her work has appeared in numerous publications. Her debut collection of poems, *Moon in my Teacup* was published by Writer's Workshop in Kolkata in 2019.

Journeys
Basudhara Roy

We, who have stayed put
in places;
hugged out of habit, reluctance,
necessity or love,
our little corners of the earth;
built and kindled
loyally for years our one hearth
of mixed blessings;
watered the same soil and
watched life
send down roots in the toil of
our nurture;

we, who are grooved
in unalterable
configurations of continuity,
we will never know
the enticement of a fresh start;
the beckoning
of impossible probabilities;
the fluidity
of translation from dreams
to possibilities.

The wonder of sunrises
and sunsets
on alien shores are not for us;
Nor the warmth
that blossoms amidst strangers
as the day
dissolves in a caress of fatigue.
We will know
less of love, lesser perhaps,
of fulfillment and loss.

And you, my friend, envy
the thickening
spindle of days that I gather
dutifully each dusk
in my chest, while you say
you must
cut the strings each night
and let
the kites of your days seek
their own destiny.

Zakir Malik is Editor-in-Chief for *ILA*, writer, and social campaigner. His recent book is titled *The Wail of the Woods*. He is also Director for UNESCO to International Youth Development Model United Nations in India, a member of the Jammu Kashmir Innovative Foundation for Transformation Society, and General Secretary for the Cultural Forum Kupwara.

The Smell of Jehlum
Zakir Malik

Thine rivers chirping from dawn till dusk
are my nights of ecstasy
from which freshness does flow
with drops of peace pouring into Dal
I hide my puzzles under your green coats,
and those glistening lilies of the Wular.

O' Kashmir you drench; glow like diamond
while my thirst quenches with balls of snow
that thatch of lush greenery
is where I belong, where I come from
rest my breaths are the guests of time.

Endless is dusk where I slide towards
slowly, slowly into the waters of Mansar,
I walk then towards Silk route to relish
and squeeze taste of nature at its best.

I live in the drops of Pangong lake
O' my land I smell your beauty
hear your voice in rush of Jehlum
see your hues in fruits and leaves.

Vietnam veteran Mark Fleisher has authored three books of poetry and collaborated on a fourth. His works have appeared in numerous online and print anthologies. Now based in Albuquerque, New Mexico, he earned a journalism degree from Ohio University.

Paper Trails
Mark Fleisher

I like grasping a newspaper,
ink smudges my fingers,
but I can wash it off
I like turning pages,
digesting the news,
good, bad, indifferent,
checking the ball scores,
chuckling at the funnies,
ranting at opinions
rendered by pompous pundits

Hold on, not so fast,
proclaim publishing poobahs
you are old hat, old school,
you and your kind,
relics from the tactile age.
better hop on the
digital bandwagon
before you're too late

Gazettes and Globes,
Posts and Presses,
Times and Tribunes,
Suns and Sentinels,
bound for museum archives
I wonder, and those names
of endangered species
gliding across the tongue
like honey butter:
the Epitaph, Vindicator,
Post-Intelligencer, Plain Dealer,
Times-Picayune,
Press-Scimitar,
the cleverly named
De Queen Bee

Poetry... The Best of 2020

Can a digital newspaper
line the bird cage,
or wrap fish,
or protect pottery
and porcelain if I move,
or soak up pee
when the cat ignores
the litter box?

I'm arrogant enough
to do crossword puzzles
in ink and sometimes it
gets messy --
that's half the fun -- can't
do that on a computer
or cell phone screen

Already I throw
disdainful looks
at folks who read
digital books
on their precious
kindles and nooks.

So sentence me
to perdition if I dare
commit sedition
reading a computerized
newspaper edition

Tyran Prizren Spahiu tries to find topics that worry, nag, excite, and embrace. To describe them is a pleasure and challenge to him. Being emotionally connected with letters, he loves a calm life and continues to spread kindness. No matter where he goes, you will hear the voice behind: "Tyran, the Bohemian was here."

The Most BEAUTIFUL FLOWER
Tyran Prizren Spahiu

. . . empress,
listen, please do listen,
it is my inner voice,
requires silence,
my being understands your happiness,
me,
I want to savor the light, say good morning, hold you,
whisper, uncover hidden feelings,
express love,
I really do,
while water waves embrace the Banks of Love,
crown inspires,
I am eager
to dance under the sounds of classical ballet,
this blessed month I have deserved,
to adorn treasure with many lyrics.

Flower Lady, the most beautiful creature,
please let me hug you calmly,
allow feelings to speak, smile arrests
eyes twist the lines of your body,
thirsty passion sings to future,
Madam,
let sincere spiritual fondness spark,
idyll, the most picturesque scene,
floating letters to breath,
you are the universe, rooted in the sentiment,
you, the Queen of the Empire.

Chijioke Ogbuike is engaged in his arts. He is a self-published poet and novelist – *Pregnant Thoughts* and *Expelled*, respectively. An independent musician, he plays under the pseudonym Ketchy Dons and has two albums – *fortune n the slave* and *A cut above the rest* to his credit. A third one is in the wings.

Here Are My Mother and My Brethren
Chijioke Ogbuike

Love is a sequence
of selections
Perhaps not very much thought of
before it happens
This also suggests alternatives
from which man makes his choice
Life came to us
with a duality
Perhaps to break the monotony
of monopoly
Life is death
as death is also life
Light is life
as darkness is also death
Fire and water
This becomes the divine path
as proclaimed in Sirach 15 v 15-18
'if you want to,
you can keep the Lord's commands.
You can decide
Whether you will be loyal to him or not.
He has placed water and fire
Before you: reach out and take whichever you want'
This is also the barometer
– 'if you want to'
Through which we select
the pebbles that defines the nature of our journey
A strange malady
has now overtaken the world
The deception of relativity
It has introduced a monkey
in our very thoughts
It now shapes
how we see our reality
Once upon a time
the bond of family was something to behold

Now parents
are merely surrogates to their children
Eighteen is a golden age
To be indoctrinated into a deceptive halloween
That soon unleashes its mayhem
on the unsuspecting and unprepared
It is a fact that those who chose us is those we also choose
Nothing is gained beyond
the certain reciprocity of payback
Most times unfortunately
family do not choose us
Or it is us perhaps
that chose not to choose family
We always prefer
the fickle breath of ambition
And the many distractions amply provided
By surfing the ether
As man continues with his destruction
of earth as nature gave it
Family faces annihilation
There is a new definition of reality
Freedom without responsibility
As we grapple with daily survival
It is also possible that our society does not choose us
It is a dog eat dog world that we are in
Everyone is not cut out of the same measure of cloth
It is inevitable that some grow up predators
Some become the victims
No one thinks of collateral damages
when the only language left is the drums of war
The choice to become immigrants
Is not always a preferred alternative
It is only an acceptance
that our home has left us forsaken
In such situation's shoulders to lean on
are looked for at distant climates
Inside geographies of ambiguities
Where the colour of your skin
Is very much a batting average

in their dubious stock exchange
At such times too, it is not always difficult to identify
Our mothers
Our brothers and sisters
Here love easily identifies those in love
Especially when we
ask for it
Look for it
Knock on its door
As we adapt to circumstances
the veil is lifted to reveal them
our mothers
our brethren
the language spoken
is usually free of ambiguity

Dilip Mohapatra, a decorated Navy Veteran from Pune, India, is a critically acclaimed poet in contemporary English. His poems regularly appear in many literary journals and anthologies worldwide. He has six poetry collections and two non-fictions to his credit.

dilipmohapatra.com

Beyond Bounds
Dilip Mohapatra

The amoeba moves up the value chain
and slides down
to come in a full circle
tracing a zero
a void
that contains all that matters
and perhaps that does not.

The singular becomes plural
in steps of ascending order
one fissions into two
the yin and yang
the duality graduates to
the trinity of triumvirates
opening the vistas
emanating in four cardinal directions
the senses and elements emerge
and the six dimensions
try to define
the boundaries of existence.

The rainbow melts and merges
into a white sheet
while you ascend along your spine
from the gross to the sublime
and run your pen
on the Möbius band
trying in vain to draw lemniscates.
The planets and the zodiac signs
dictating your destiny
you continue your
search for synchronicity
unendingly.

Till perhaps you realize that
the drop engulfs the ocean
the void envelopes the universe
and the zero confines infinity.

June Barefield, AKA June Bugg, is a budding anarchist, military veteran, and a proud father of three. He has authored three collections of poetry, and enjoys reading, the outdoors – mostly sunrises, and makes a swell pot of rice and beans too!

Help Me
June Barefield, AKA June Bugg

Anchored firmly here on the bottom
Tethered heavenly here
on
the
BOTTOM

My dream requisite ingestible
An acquired taste
My fate & destiny manifest too late
Here in this place
On the bottom where i deconstruct my hate

Help me!
My fear & doubt impregnate some goofy dream deferred
A raisin in the sun ignored
Always

I Keep one eYe on the bourgeois
Witness do i another deplorable compromise restored

Help me!
Here
On the
Bottom
Again ignored

Skim do eYe lightly over the absurd
Here
On the
Bottom
Where i must choose
My choice a trap infused
I be not confused
It matters not
I Choose a choice already chosen 4 me
Generational my choice

Assimilated into the asylum
Nurtured in the fantastifical!
Help me define my voice

Help me!

My inferiority is a complex
A germ
Worming its way thru all the limits of my ambivalence
Conditioned by blind, raging, indifference
Indifferent
Here
On the
Bottom
Reaching deeply down into the bloody red toil enriching the soil
& for the sake of the cause, unawares, i adopt the process
Whitened by years and years of humiliation
Not My process

Inflexible 2 kneeling i must kneel
Kneel at the altar of my abasement
Here on the bottom i inoculate this feeling, concealing nothing
Here on the bottom i dig my heels viciously into the flanks of a world not made 4 me

I watch
& i wait
My patience a slave
Here on the bottom tethered heavenly

Help me
Please.

D' Siafa Draper is a native of Liberia. A survivor of a 14-year civil war, he experienced the struggles and inequalities of being a refugee. His writings cut across love, spirituality, world peace and the politics of Africa. He believes that life may not be lovely, but it is lovable.

Reflections from the Rear
D' Siafa Draper

Solemn and vast is the opened field
Obscured in dooms of nights out of sight

Ceramic bodies scrapped off life's essence, woven in rags
Unease bodies shoveled down as sunset plunges into eternity

Echoes of mournful souls combs our streets
Abandoning quieted bodies in clays and tombs

Weeping softly, seeking independence
From the claws of death – the highest bidder

Alas

Wrestling glens of darkness to greet the morning sun
They'd wished to live their youthfulness –

Free from the chains of enforced slavery
A kind of freedom that condemns clutches injustice

But now dines in company of distress
Each so depressed residing in homes of defective lights

Denied the kiss of mercy, victimized by bomb mines
No metaphor to express heart's grievances reminisced

Now each standing firm in painful silence
With spoken words unheard, as each night might be bitter or better

Vain in harvest must each soul reap
Like a crimson rose one trampled ground

Life's battles never won
Silent souls linger here and there

Wandering bones without homes
As empty tombs become swimming pools

Solemn and vast is the opened field
Obscured in dooms of nights out of sight

Monsif Beroual is an internationally renowned poet from Morocco. He has received multiple awards, including "The World Icon of Literature of the National Academy of Arts and Culture" (India, 2020) and "The Pablo Neruda Medal" (2017). He is the Youth Ambassador of Morocco for Inner Child Press International.

The Heart of a Poet
Monsif Beroual

In this humanity sake journey
I'll be like Jean Piaget
When he starts seeing the world
Through a child's heart
Or like Alexis Tocqueville when he decides
To walk in this endless road
To reach American Democracy
Or like Charles Wright Mills, who establish the politics of truth
Through the promise
To be honest and pure no matter how will be the cost,
And like Spinoza who takes the magic stare from the universe
To unchains a hidden truth
Or like Friedrich Nietzsche
When he screamed loud: "Zardach, God is dead!"
When he discovered the world is getting colder.
And I wished over all ends or starts within philosophy's heart
May our world be embraced by love song again.

Alicia Minjarez Ramírez, a translator and an internationally renowned Mexican poet, has won numerous prizes, including "The World Cultural Excellence Award" (2020, from the government of Peru), "The Excellence Prize World Poetry Championship" (2019, Romania), and "The EASAL Medal Award (2018, from The European Academy of Sciences and Letters, France).

Blue Whispers
Alicia Minjarez Ramírez

Freezing raindrops
Pour hasty voices
Over my body,
leaving behind
Fragmented unfinished moments,
In the dense night of my foliage.

Amber lights crystallize
Wet cobblestones.
Faint breeze throbs tactile words
In ragweed of your lips.

The wind impels
Among its branches
Lost – found longings
Inside the indigo ink of your gaze,
As silent opacity shimmer flashes
Delimit folds of the shining water
Running down my cheeks.
Should I hear the breeze pronounce your name?

Blue whispers articulate
Songs of the stones.
Pierced transparencies dissolve desires,
As melts the stone with the fire
And the sea on the horizon.

From Bangladesh, Kamrul Islam is Professor of English. He is a bilingual poet who has eleven books of poems to his credit. He has been honored by the Gujarat Sahitya Academy and the Motivational Strips on India's 74th Independence Day. His poetic work appeared in different national and international magazines.

An Exuberant Virgin Butterfly
Kamrul Islam

Treading the shattered dreams,
I traverse the woods and gentle trees
To know the tales of birds' music.

Old leaves cuddle the new to bring
The milieu of vernal grace,
The clouds move with brilliant moods,
The doctors search for words spent
To mend the scars and wounds of souls.

Peace and love, the magical wand,
The scintillating way for greater bond
To surmount the odds and worldly pains.

Not utopia, an exuberant virgin butterfly,
Wings of spectacular divine colors,
Shows the blissful road to walk on . . .

Poetry... The Best of 2020

Langley Shazor was raised in Bristol, Virginia. He has a deep appreciation for culture, arts, wellness, history, philosophy, science, religions, and education. Writing is not only personally therapeutic for the author, but a medium for which he has the opportunity to impart positivity on those from all walks of life.

A Rarified Breed
Langley Shazor

Killing fields scattered
Marrow-ed remains
Of carbon-based lifeforms
Disregarded and discarded
By domestic poachers
Set on display
Viewed and never assisted
Does not everything hath has life
Also have a soul?
On the verge of cultural extinction
These existential eccentricities
Breed fear and lathing
For real life melodrama
Documentaries, discussions, dialogue
Develop drastically varying perceptions
With unifying positions
If I have not yet begun the fight
Have I already been predetermined
To death?
We all return to ash
Unintended to be prematurely snuffed out
Exhale this anatomical animosity
And let us all
Breathe

Kashiana Singh resides in Chicago where her life embodies her TEDx Talk theme, "Work as Worship". In her poetry collection, *Shelling Peanuts and Stringing Words*, she speaks as a participant and an observer. Her chapbook, *Crushed Anthills* is a journey through 10 cities. Kashiana's poems have been published on various platforms.

The Country
Kashiana Singh

When did you stop listening; become unwilling to look up; look away from your own opiate limbs; look away from birthmarks on your skin; look away from the falling blisters of your eyes;

When did you become so lazy that you let the claws of your feet burrow deep, trapped in your own blemished ground; unmoving even when being eaten alive—
by the blooming anguish of your people; by odors from floating carcasses of your soul; by the waves that beat against the sunken scales of your ghosts; by sordid drippings of pleas fleeing your own mouth.

At this very moment I am a lighthouse standing in watch; I am carving my solitary light into ripples; each ripple a caterpillar pupating; a butterfly pulsating to panchkritya1 of tandav dance; its wings flapping to the spitting fire of a trillion monarchs; unwilling to diapause until you listen to the whistling of their alliterative song.

They will circle you into an orchestrated garland, evacuating your cauldron of prayers, and pledges, until you hear their buzzing silence; they will drink incessantly of your matted milkweed, they will churn intemperate until you hear anew.

For if you don't; an apocalypse is coming closer and closer towards your shore; you have time now to gaze outwards and listen; to act before being engulfed into the whirlpool of growling stillness; to become the country we knew.

To become the country, we knew.

Teresa E. Gallion is on a spiritual journey, traveling and hiking mountain and desert landscapes. She has three books to her credit: *Walking Sacred Ground*, *Contemplation in the High Desert*, and *Chasing Light* – a finalist in the 2013 New Mexico/Arizona Book Awards. Her work has appeared in numerous journals and anthologies.

http://teresagallion.yolasite.com/

Plea for Unity
Teresa E. Gallion

Brothers and sisters of planet earth,
we must breathe in rhythm to the harmony
of the earth rotating.

Earth is tilting in her axis from the weight
of negative energy and physical destruction.
We are destined to fall into the unknown

with no name in the universe unless
we learn to breathe out love together.
It is only through the compassionate gift

of kindness to one another that love
is manifest and peace may flow like
a mighty river from our souls.

We may continue our battles to see
who will be temporary king of the hill
or we may choose to send love notes
to the universe.

A call for prayer, gratitude and forgiveness
is needed to show the human race values
the privilege of living on planet earth.

Louise Hudon was born in 1951 in Trois-Rivière, Québec with the soul of a poet. She is known for her ballads and poetic texts published in multiple volumes. She has over 680 poems read worldwide.

www.louisehudonmedium.com

The Importance of Life
Louise Hudon

Have you reached your darkest steps?
Your tears run dry?
Black clouds are on the horizon
Worsening the state of your prison?

If you are surrounded by the darkness of life,
Dream of the sun and for its return
We are not bound by evil
After the rain, there will be a rainbow.

Leave your heart and mind open with nature.
Forget your debts and bills
The recipe for life
Is to feel one's spirituality.

Do not dismiss your past wisdom.
For it helps you surpass yourself.
In the quest for happiness,
Put in all your effort, never despair

While I wait, my writings will free me
And with the help of angels, I rely on my wits.
I want to come to your aid.
With hope that your spirit will rise once again.

We support you, my friend, did you know?
I noticed you looking disheartened
Understanding your inner suffering.
We shall heal you with our best wishes.

Edited by Kayla Trottier on September 17th, 2020

Suranjit Gain was born on October 8, 1984 in the Khulna district of Bangladesh. He received his education in Bangladesh and India, and is being congratulated by the universe in the field of literature.

The Child-Teenage
Suranjit Gain

We are children
innocent like flower;
blessing of god,
clean our character.

New born-teenage-lad,
we are in future;
build up country and
life chariot's driver.

The sun of knowledge
our little heart;
will shine the universe,
it's true must.

Little sands
create continent;
we are small but
infinite life in breast.

New day's dreams
play in our eyes;
we are joyful sky,
river's waves nice.

Dewy green field,
morning sun-shine;
we are like ocean,
unique and fine.

Our smile fresh
as dawn wind;
weeping brings dark,
as set of sun kind.

Poetry... The Best of 2020

We are more nice
to lap of mother;
make joyful house
sweet talking of ours.

Poets of the World

The poet Rajashree Mohapatra writes in Odia and English. Her poems have been translated into many languages. Her poems appeared in international anthologies, e-zines and journals. She has co-authored two poetry books: *Mirage* and *Seeker*. She devotes her time to painting. She has studied the traditional paintings of Odisha as a source of history.

There She Is . . .
Rajashree Mohapatra

Where wind streams amid the hills
Upon the boughs , cherries shine
There angels sing to reveal mysteries
A joy, filled in rain drops silently drizzles.

There you find a budding rose
Sovereign of beauty,
Under the heaven as she grows
An earthly flower, smiles on throne

Glorious days carve verses
Upon the strand they are engraved
Inlay of desires with gold and gems
Emeralds melt to ivory waves

There she rises from her blissful bed
Between shadow and light to reign
When she sings , music is still
In her note, you breathe soulful glee.

Like the sun she is ever new
every morning, a refreshing dew.
Her dreams dance in meadows green
She is there . . .
With her songs of love eternal yet divine.

Poets of the World

Nguyen Chau Ngoc Doan Chinh, AKA Hong Ngoc Chau (Nguyen Chinh on FB), hails from Vietnam. She holds a Master's degree in Education Management and a diploma from Premio Mundial A La Excelencia Literary 2019-2020. She won the Copper Cross of The World Union Of Poets for Promotion of Art in 2020.

Mother's Words Spoken to Her Daughter
Nguyen Chau Ngoc Doan Chinh, AKA Hong Ngoc Chau

LỜI MẸ NÓI VỚI CON GÁI

Con gái thân yêu nghe mẹ dạy
Đời con một nửa sống bên người
Chứ không còn bé trong tay mẹ
Nuôi nấng chở che mãi không thôi.

Sẽ có một ngày con nghĩ đến
Trước tiên con nghĩ đến người kia
Chứ không là mẹ còn ôm ấp
Âu yếm vui buồn cùng sẻ chia

Sẽ chẳng giản đơn, con gái nhé
Trái tim con bắt đầu bâng khuâng
Băn khoăn về một điều gì khác
Mẹ hiểu, con yêu! Điều thiết thân

Mẹ chẳng thể nào mà trói buộc
Con yêu người bạn trai yêu con
Lại càng không thể ngăn con đạt
Giữ những lời thề hẹn núi non.

Mẹ chỉ xem người con lựa chọn
Góp phần ý kiến hay cùng con
Về điều nhỏ nhặt đời thường nhất
Yêu được người là một chiến công

Con phải gắng công nhiều lắm đó
Người đời thường nói phở và cơm
Đồ ăn so sánh với con gái
Sao phải nghĩ mình là phở cơm

Con phải là con – người phụ nữ
Mà trong ánh mắt người đàn ông
Đàn bà đơn giản gồm hai loại
Loại để yêu và loại . . . để không.

Nếu chẳng được yêu, đừng dự trữ
Con không nên có nhiều nhân tình
Không lo con thiếu người con chọn
Mẹ chẳng yêu cầu con đẹp xinh

Học rộng tài cao giỏi đủ việc
Mẹ mong, con hãy tìm ra tiền
Tự do tài chính là cần thiết
Cố gắng làm nên sự nhản tiền

Giàu có bao nhiêu, con nhất quyết
Cũng không ỷ lại, vững tinh thần
Cho dù con giỏi hơn người đó
Đừng để người yêu thấy tủi thân

Đừng ngạo mạn tiền con kiếm được
Vô nghì khi đặt lên bàn cân
Mối quan hệ buộc con gìn giữ
Phụ nữ cần trân trọng đối phương.

Đôi lúc đàn ông cũng tội nghiệp
Chỉ vì không biết những điều cần
Giận hờn chi đó, con bình tĩnh
Đừng cố tỏ ra con quá căng

Họ nhẫn không như con đã nghĩ
Nhiều khi họ giống trẻ thơ ngây
To thân, lớn xác, nhưng ngờ nghệch
Con cũng mềm, già néo đứt dây

Hai đứa trẻ con tình sẽ vỡ.
Trưởng thành lên, đến lúc rồi con
Họ cần con gái điều gì nhỉ!
Con phải làm gì con biết không?

Là quen nhưng chẳng hề nhàm chán
Sẻ chia nhưng chớ để cam tâm
Họ không là của riêng con nhé

Đừng có chủ quan, mắc lỗi lầm

Gắng sức để làm người phụ nữ
Tài ba, mẹ nghĩ là không nên.
Không ai có thể hoàn toàn cả!
Tủ kính búp bê đứng một bên

Cao quá thì không ai dám với
Khiêm nhu vị trí con nơi đâu
Là ai tự biết, khôn ngoan nhất
Cố vẽ hư danh sẽ lộ sau.

Càng vẽ khác chi đeo mặt nạ.
Con không giấu mãi mối đuôi đầu
Việc nhà tị nạnh con không giúp
Chắc chắn có ngày sẽ tuyệt giao

Bình đẳng nữ nam ai cũng biết
Thương con họ hiểu cách hài hòa
Đừng nên câu nệ, quá sòng phẳng..
Mới giữ được người đó ở nhà.

Nghe mẹ, con thường xuyên nấu nướng
Những ngày sóng gió ập thuyền con
Thủy chung là thứ mẹ căn dặn.
Tay nắm tay, đừng vội bỏ buông.

Vì có người đã từng nuối tiếc
Lỡ duyên, bạc phận trách ông Trời
Con nên khôn khéo biết hòa thuận
Mẹ nghĩ rằng con hạnh phúc thôi.

Mother's Words Spoken to Her Daughter
Nguyen Chau Ngoc Doan Chinh, AKA Hong Ngoc Chau

Listen to my teaching, my dear girl!
Half of your life you'll live with another
You're still not young, being nurtured
And protected by my arms forever

There will be a day you have a romance
First of all, you think of a young man
Not to think of your mother embracing you
Caressing you to share sadness and joy clues

It will not be simple, my dear girl
Your heart will begin to wander
To be worried about another secrecy
I understand, my girl! The necessaries

I cannot bind you – cannot forbid you
To love your boyfriend who loves you
I cannot even stop you to obtain
Your vow with rivers and mountains

I only consider your chosen lover
For contributing my sincere ideas
About things small in normal life
Loving a young man is a good surprise

You have to contemplate a lot in mind
People usually, analyze noodle and rice
Alas! How is food to compare with girls?
Why do you think yourself to be noodles or rice?

You must be yourself – a woman
Or a kind girl in the eyes of a man
Simply, he divided girls into two kinds
A kind for being loved . . . another for bye

If not being loved, don't keep anyone
You should not have many loving ones
Don't worry to lack a man for your choice
You're so beautiful I don't like to require

You mustn't be widely talent, good at all jobs
But you can make money as I always hope
Never depend on anyone on money – never!
Try to make money - a before-eye matter

Although having much money, please decide
Not to rely on it, let be stable your mind
Although you earn more money than he'll do
Don't let your lover feels ashamed. It's true

Don't be proud of your money earning
When putting on the scale it means nothing
It's an obligatory relationship you must keep
A woman needs to respect a life partnership

For a sincere man, he's occasionally pitied
Only because he doesn't know necessaries
If you are in anger, let be calm, in the end
Don't try to show your heavy discontent

He isn't patient as you think, I remind
He sometimes looks like a naïve child
Of course, he has a big body but he's still silly
Be soft, everything has its broken point truly

If two of you are childish, love will be broken
Be an adult, you are at the mature age golden
Dear girl! What he needs you to do, please show!
You must be a serious person, do you know?

You are familiar with him but not boring
You may share but it's not your burdening
Before marriage, he is not your own sake
Don't be subjective, you'll make mistakes

Poets of the World

If you try to be a good talented woman
I think you should not be in such romance
No one is perfect everyone naturally knows
Don't be a beautiful doll in the glass window

If you're high talent no one dares to love you
You should humble to see your position true
For you to know yourself, It will be wiser
You try to show off, the bad fame appears

If you show off, it means you wear a mask
You cannot hide your personal clue at last
The housework you are envious not to do
Surely there will be a break up of you two

Among people, they all know the equality
Loving you he knows how to harmony
Do not be draconian or extremely fair
So you can keep him be at home there

Obey me, do your cooking frequently
During the stormy days in your family
Loyalty is the thing you have to keep
Hand in hand, you don't rush to leave

There has ever been someone to regret already
She blamed God due to ungraceful, unlucky destiny
You should be smart to get along more or less
I really think you will be in your happiness . . .

Attracta Fahy, a psychotherapist [. . .], lives in Co, Galway. She holds an M.A. in Writing and authored a chapbook, *Dinner in the Fields*. The October winner in *Irish Times* [. . .] and a Pushcart [. . .] nominee, she was shortlisted for Over The Edge New Writer [. . .].

Do It
Attracta Fahy

(*After Charles Bukowski*)

If you are going to try, go all the way,
do it, do it, do it, do it, and I did.
I went all the way down to five and a half stone,
doing it.

All the way to bone, shedding my body,
ultimately yours, stamps, stickers,
imprints, impressions, what to be,
who not to be.

I sunk into the deep,
took my anger, its sword of discernment,
love, a lantern to light shadowy guts.

In this body, bind and wound
were one, like ivy clings to trees,
all bound in hunger.
Everybody became everybody's shadow.

I sunk into death, its bloodied waters,
insatiable starvation in protest wanted more,
and more, to be less, and less, and less again.

A world with blinded eyes refused.
I smashed their convex image,
turned the stone which formed these bones,
the murky underworld,
shady maggots, snails, and ants, coiled in dark.
I clawed my way up from there.

Supratik Sen is a blogger who writes fiction, non-fiction, poems in Bengali – his mother tongue, in English, and in French. His writings have appeared in numerous anthologies and magazines.

It's You
Supratik Sen

Morning dew
Falls in my eyes,
Another sunrise
Will be seen
In the horizon,
A pack of lies
Will begin to
Consume the day,
Alluring ways,
Mad rush, chasing time,
Ignoring the rising star
For a meaningless reason,
Will invariably lead
The world and its cousin
To the pre-written prison.

In the interim,
Let me hum
With the birds,
Without words.

I wonder how sadness
Can be so beautiful,
It brings us closer
To the truth.

I realize that the dew
Is not just a mere drop,
It's your presence, it's you.

Poetry... The Best of 2020

From Siliguri, Darjeeling, Zinia Mitra teaches English at the University of North Bengal. Her poems have appeared in national and international journals, including *Muse India*, *Ruminations*, *Contemporary Literary Review*, *Kavya Bharati*, *East Lit. Indian Literature*, *Coldnoon*, *Asian Signature*, *Teesta Review*, *Setu*, *Pangolin Review*, and *Poetry Potion*.

Lag
Zinia Mitra

Lag is failure to keep up with others
in a movement or a development;
a period of time between one event and another;
a retardation in an electric current flow ;
also another term for string
(North American billiards)*
-strings tie up
our bits and pieces when we lag behind.
It is a harrowing feeling of exclusion
like a torn scrunched page that lands outside the bin
or like the silence of time when a companion has hired a sturdy boat and left the curved shores of life
and we grow conscious of the dead wet sand under our feet
and question the meaninglessness of the oblong bubbles of water that pop up.

Sometimes it is pleasant to lag behind
when all the others with their backpacks have hurried away
to look at the crumpled bed sheets, used towels and lipstick-stained coffee cups
to imagine their very very busy sunlit days.

Sometimes it is wonderful to lag behind
in a relationship when the other has moved away
listen to old songs, feel the dog- eared books, smile at the photographs
and imagine the fresh tapering fingers of friendship holding his hand.
Sometimes I lag behind to savor these fine moments
to know that I exist. Always alone.

* Definitions from Oxford Languages, online

Uwe Friesel, a published author and translator (Nabokov and Updike, among others), was the first president of the Unified German Writers Union (VS) after 1989; co-organizer of Writers' Cruises in the Baltic and Aegean Seas, and co-founder of the international UNESCO-Centers in Visby and Rhodes. His rewards include Villa Massimo Rome, Writer-in-Residence Hamburg and Berlin, and German Literature Fonds.

http://www.uwefriesel.de/art_nouveau.html

Ewigkeitsgedicht
Uwe Friesel

Der Winter ist vergangen
Die Bäume grünen noch
Die güldnen Sternlein prangen
Rund um ein Schwarzes Loch

Das Weltall es verschwindet
Und schafft sich dann stets neu
Nur unsre kleine Erde
Hat immer Gott dabei

Eternity-Poem
Uwe Friesel

Winter now has vanished
Trees are getting green
Golden stars replenish
Black holes gape in between

The universe is shrinking
To mighty nothingness
Just tiny earth keeps blinking
In GOD's own fussy mess

The poems of Akash Sagar are a part of numerous anthologies and poetry festivals, including Efflorescence by Chennai Poetry Circle, Glomag by Glory Sasikala, The Virtual Reality (Sparrow Publishers), and Guntur Int. Poetry Fest. He is a proud member of Soul Scriber's Society of Salem that organizes the annual Yercaud Poetry Festival.

Inner Interrogation
Akash Sagar

Four directions strand
vagabonding on nomadic lands
alas! Who resides within?
inner interrogation.

Elements five unrecognize
Fibonacci senses comprehend sky
alas! What ignites within?
inner interrogation.

119 atoms on table
molecules react in fables
alas! Where were all these within?
inner interrogation.

Calendars color days
mélange march different ways
alas! Why flags numbers within?
inner interrogation.

Born in Jerusalem, Israel, Channah Moshe grew up in Western Europe. Writing is her nirvana. Her poems have been published in the US, the UK, India, Italy and on the Internet. Her hobbies include photography, ballroom dancing, homeopathy, baking, reading, writing, and feeding stray cats.

A Picture
Channah Moshe

On the backdrop
of sand dunes
and turquoise waters
an opulent man
and stunning woman
sit at a cafe
with two teenagers
munching
chatting
and laughing.

What a picture!

As one of the teenagers
I can reveal
it is as much
a fata morgana
as the desert
can produce.

For she is not his wife
the teenage daughters
his only
when he returns
from yet another
escapade overseas
and the laughing
hides the tension
that in a snap
it might all
evaporate.

Poets of the World

Armenuhi Sisyan, from Armenia, has 10 books to her credit (the last 2 were published in Japanese in Kyoto). Her work has been translated into 13 languages. She is a member of different writers' associations across the world, has participated in various international literary festivals and programs, and received several international literary prizes.

Sometimes
Armenuhi Sisyan

The angels sometimes
are dying to see something
that is not theirs-
they get punished:
the curiosity burns their wings a little
and they get depleted
sometimes . . .
The angels want sometimes
to be in places where they shouldn't be,
and their feet hits the ground
Instead of blood – pain oozes from their feet,
and they struggle to go forward,
sometimes . . .
The angels want to try things sometimes
not belonging them
and they almost lose themselves,
so the sky oozes from their eyes . . .
Maybe the angels need to be forgiven
Sometimes . . .?

Poets of the World

Maria Do Sameiro Barroso (Portugal), is a medical doctor, a multilingual poet, translator, researcher, and an essayist. Her poetry books have been published in several countries and were awarded prestigious literary prizes. Her poems appeared in over one hundred national and international literary magazines and anthologies in over twenty languages.

Cosmogony
Maria Do Sameiro Barroso

In the beginning, a large empty flower
began to stir.
We were the earth and the sky,
moving in the shade.
In our story, there were birds,
mountains and haze.
Like Spring sprouts, we started
moving across the sun and the rainbows.
In the slime of shells and corals,
I heard your first words,
not knowing how to stop the purple,
the rivers, the sky,
or the yellow flower of the sun violins.
We were born out of a sweet
cosmogony.
We came to each other
out of a rebellious desire,
playing an ancient game,
reviving an enchanting spell
by the quietness of a river,
the shadow of white poplars,
listening to the gorgeous sound
of a well-tuned lyre.

Jyoti Nair, a Learning and Development Professional, works for a top-level Indian MNC as the Capability Development Manager for global HR Operations. Her writings have appeared in Indian journals, anthologies and e-zines. She aims to harness the power of her pen, championing for social issues such as child abuse and mental health awareness.

Oneiric Peekaboo
Jyoti Nair

I borrowed the oneiric lenses from Morpheus last night.
For I had to wear my wings and leap into the Elysian atmosphere.
Hark! I have alighted, and there's already a star carpet spread for each who arrives.
A Chalice is placed at the center, and I am told that it contains the stardust philtre.
It is the welcome drink for us, the languid travelers who have enrolled
    for this peekaboo game.
Verily, I am being captured by the dewy mistiness of the reticle, the cosmos shutterbug
    waving from atop.
Unequivocally, I am enveloped in a diaphanous garb, I felt I am swinging in a
    waterfall hammock.
There are a plethora of seasons to walk into, the seasonal embellishments
    nudge each door as signboards.
I am still flummoxed, should I opt for clementine clad autumn or
    burnished blossoming spring?
I wish for the ballerina pumps to foxtrot between both the celestial vales.
Suddenly a vehement voice reverberates,
"we have only one protocol, eliminate greed if you want to stay".
I step back, I feel washed and cleansed by that resounding grasp.
Unruffled, I remove the borrowed lenses and scamper to pick my poem-diary.
This time, I didn't have to keep doodling to zero-in the besotting title.
The title is 'Uprooting Pleonexia',
I slide the window blinds to inhale the tangerine pollens of the refurbished day.
I dunk into the poetic vessel, steering my choked Euphemisms into those orbits...
Where ink unleashes its wanderlust valves.
Where my funambulist mind dares to plunge,
Into the unbeknown terrains.

From Russia, Galina Italyanskaya is a former pediatrician and molecular biologist, who now works as an English teacher. She has been writing poetry since her childhood. Some of her poems appeared in poetry anthologies, such as *Poets Unite Worldwide* by Fabrizio Frosini and *Our Poetry Archive* by NilavroNill Shoovro.

The Crown
Galina Italyanskaya

Kings of the earth, don't be so blind!
Don't lose your poor mind!
The crown of Death is shining bright,
His mantle spreads behind.

Its scarlet baize with black and white
Has covered the world.
Kings of the earth, do stop your fight,
Wars in the name of gold!

While the pandemic's splashing wide,
The globe is getting sick,
You, cunning people, keep in sight
It makes your foes weak.

For people's lives without sleep
They're fighting night and day,
But six feet under is too deep
And late to keep away.

You want to benefit from it
Just to secure your thrones.
Kings of the earth, restrain your greed!
You're dancing on the bones!

Still, it's not you who calls the tune.
Get real! It's not your ball!
Nobody knows, but maybe soon
Your own crowns will fall.

Sayak Bhandari is a teaching professional in Eastern India. He is a postgraduate in English Literature and Environmental Studies. He has been working painstakingly in the restoration of wildlife and biodiversity. He also works for school dropouts who are exploited in industries. He is a passionate traveler and visual storyteller.

Estranged
Sayak Bhnadari

We shall meet. Surely shall we . . .

We shall meet in the plague's aftermath,
When the depressing documents of destruction
Are buried behind the fatal fences.
After perishing mortal remains,
Turn just into a number;
And are kept stockpiled in an aircon dead room,
Or even in some bloody cesspool nearby.

When gay footfalls
Bless the happy autumn fields again.
We shall meet. Surely shall we . . .

We shall meet when the feisty fight
Fought with every sob and plight,
Is finally done.
When man defeats its invisible enemy,
A deadly foe, strangely silent.

When psyche is sanitized to sanity,
And the sleepless paranoid eyes relaxed.
We shall meet. Surely shall we . . .

We shall meet as the medicos smile
Once the ceaseless combat is over.
We shall meet as a compendious statesman
Pats on my back with no frowned face.
When ugly dark shackles,
And fear's tentacles
Succumb to the lucent hue of human force.
Let's win over our shaky feet,
Let's meet in the clamours of crowded street,
Let's meet the way we always did.

Poets of the World

Maryam Abbasi finds words to be alive and breathing as any human being. She learned to feel the emotions within them before she learned to express them [. . .]. An academic and a student, Maryam tries to inculcate passion for literature in young hearts and minds she is shaping.

Count the Cycle
Maryam Abbasi

Period 1: Enchantment

The first description of poetry came out of the word
'Blood'
All red, all gruesome; for a thirteen-year-old to eat and fathom
But isn't that how your first heartbreak turns into an apocalypse
Turns
you into a witch; your soul haunted.

Period 2: Denouncement

Words started to turn into verbs more than nouns
A city too loud; A voice too bleak in the vast crowd
Feelings stung; touching a new body and calling it holy
Rose amongst the screams, a prose; all too silent; all too virgin
A little moan released, not knowing it was devoid of saying , 'please'

Period 3: Memory

Seeing across, a vision stalks
A picture too alike; A feeling too naive
The corridors have echoes again of laughter; of slaughters done behind closed eyes
Watching a step or two and you find
A picture of your youth,
All dressed in skin and bone
Drinking a cocktail of words smeared in blood and ink
Looking straight into your eyes
Calling you 'mama' with YOUR borrowed wicked smile.

Gabriela Nikoloska was born on August 6, 1999 in the city of Prilep in Macedonia. She has completed her secondary vocational education in Prilep. Nikoloska is engaged in writing prose and poetry.

The smell of your hair
Gabriela Nikoloska

I see you from afar
how do you stand and
you melt my heart.
I admire you
of your beauty
on your beautiful and kind face,
on your eyes that
they enchant my gaze on you.
I smile at you
but you do not notice me.
And finally when it passed
beside me
I smelled it
your hair smell
which left me speechless.

Poets of the World

Mourad Faska is an aspiring Moroccan researcher, a featured poet, a writer, and an essayist. His literary interests range across Gothic literature, Magic Realism, Science Fiction and Fantasy, ancient mythology, and peace-seeking literature, to name a few. He is currently working on a full-length poetry collection.

Time Flies
Mourad Faska

Time flies
Like a falling star
With no beginning or end,
Measured by the human mind,
But is never felt.
Time flies like
The blowing wind,
With no beginning or end,
elusive and incomprehensible,
Rootless, yet inevitable.
Time's a word
That suffered
A sea change,
With no beginning or end.

Tihomir Jancovski, born in 1967 in Skopje, Macedonia, is a writer and translator. He is considered as one of the most widely-read poets in his country. Thus far, he has eleven books of poetry and two novels to his credit. His literary work has been translated into 15 languages.

For Sale
Tihomir Jancovski

We were sitting at a white table
In the atelier
On wooden armchairs
He and I
And our demons

The painter in him
Transitioned from
Painting on rectangular surfaces
To painting on triangular objects
Some of them are smooth and beautiful
Almost like women

What's new?
The air purifier.
Not the dog, he's two.

I asked him and he told me
He's selling everything on the walls,
On the floor, he's not getting attached
To his paintings or past times
Pieces of furniture, monkeys
Birds, people, fish
Or obsessions

If someone wants it,
I will send him the fire
Someone will know how to dismantle it
From all the things in the room,
Only the soul is not for sale.

Dr. Varsha Das, former Director of National Book Trust, India, served as the Director of National Gandhi Museum following her retirement. She writes fiction, non-fiction, poetry, radio plays and for children in Gujarati, Hindi and English, and translates from Bangla, English, Gujarati, Hindi, Marathi and Odia. Her poems appeared in several anthologies in India and abroad.

The Sky
Varsha Das

I thought I was the coveted serene tranquil blue sky
and was happy with my transparent light body
But at night I turned dark, opaque n heavy
in which the moon and the stars shone brightly!

As the day broke, I turned vermillion
and at noon, burning yellow.
Am I changing my clothes so fast?
Or I have no clothes, so no colour can last!

Dust particles and the sun paint me,
adorn me even with the rainbow,
I am admired till the rainbow fades,
what a transient existence I have!

To be frank, I am an everlasting vast space,
anyone can cut across me with ease,
birds, balloons, planes, rockets, shooting stars . . . anything,
Because I'm all embracing space, indeed!

Poets of the World

Joseph S. Spence, Sr., a retired U.S. Army officer, has authored ten poetry books, and conceived the "Epulaeryu Poetry", "Linking Pin Sonnet", and "Trilogy Poetry" forms. His writings were published globally. He taught at Bryant and Stratton universities, and is a Goodwill Ambassador. He resides in Wisconsin, USA.

Trilogy of Non-Violence Advocates:
Rev. Dr. King, Jr., Attys. Mandela and Gandhi!
Joseph S. Spence, Sr.

An uplifting spirit of the "Trilogy of Non-Violence" advocates justice for humanity
Humanity uplifting to behold another avenue of overcoming the real struggle of life.
Life, where all souls are valuable and are fighting alongside love to overcoming hate
Hate, which the Reverend Dr. Martin Luther King Jr. states, is "Driven out by the light."
The light-giving all hearts inspirational insight with the dawn of the embolden sun.
Sun on the resurrection, the spirituality of non-violence being victorious over violence!

Sun awakening the world with its golden rays of brightness—eliminating darkness
Darkness, which Attorney Nelson Mandela survived in the dark gloomy dungeons.
Dungeons the bastions of South African apartheid established to suppress humanity
Suppress humanity by using isolation, to rent his spirit and soul without any relent
Relent, he withstood and overcame with God's grace and not seeking revenge.
Revenge, he states, "Violence, does only one thing--breeds counter-violence!"

Violence develops turmoil in the mind, body, soul, and spirit—"Sincerely agonizing!"
Agonizing the spirit to attempt ailing actions toward others and uplifting violence.
Violence Attorney Mahama Gandhi pronounced is inferior to nonviolence!
Nonviolence is innate strength emanating from the indomitable spirit of humanity.
Humanity, he states, "Died in vain if Jesus did not teach us to regulate life by love."
His Satyagraha philosophy held, "The truth of nonviolence brings independence!"

Lovingly: unity, humanity, and dignity rightly proliferate—"International Advocacy!"
Advocacy erasing images of the beast displaying an ugly appearance—they advocated.
The Rev. Dr. King Jr., Attorneys Mandela, and Bapu Gandhi defeating such ugliness!
The "Trilogy of Non-Violence," uplifting the spirit of humanity with inspiring resiliency
Resiliency showing the world how good overcame evil—"The essence of Diwali."
God's glorious resurrection will always overcome violent crucifixions—Nonviolently!

Poets of the World

Raed Anis Al-Jishi is an award-winning poet and a translator from Qateef, Saudi Arabia. He has an honorary fellowship in Writing from Iowa University (U.S.A.). He is a member of the Advisory Committee of Exquisite Teacher Training program at the National Changua University of Education (Taiwan), and an editor for *Modern Dialogs* (Macedonia).

The Peak
Raed Anis Al-Jishi

Why do you think of another peak
when you summit your own mountain,
and why do you become infected by vanity
and practice laughing
while there is no one to listen
to the flight of Ecstasy.

Lionizing is a naive social creature;
in loneliness, laughing become nothing but a buzz.

Your foot is still touching the dirt,
and the peak is not an ideal end
for a superior variety.

The peak is the starting line in the race --

You just need to smile and feel
the vitality.

You will leap and bet on flying
with all the weight of your letters.

And what if you fall? Your soul
won't touch the desert.

And your body will reach its highest condition while it is falling,
crushed by the humility of your bones against nature.

The air feels you;
drizzle wishes to write your blood's Iliad
and feels proud when it reads it
and asks itself: is it really me
who wrote the elegy of bleeding?

Reading is rewriting after liberation
from the Obsession of membranes.

It is a pure framing for the last jump --
a frame, but a part of the intimacy of creation.

Iwu Jeff is a Nigerian creative writer and instructor of English and literature. His literary works have appeared in literary magazines and anthologies, including the previous anthologies of the Inner Child Press International. He has authored a play, *Verdict of the Gods* and a novel, *Files of the Heart*.

I Died
Iwu Jeff

I died the day I saw an angel in the eye of the sun,
gleaming with light for warmth,
clothed in love and trust,
arms outstretched for sweet embrace.

But it wasn't an angel I saw,
it was Lucifer falling from the sky,
masked like a robber,
knowing no flesh. No blood.
No kith. No kin.
Burning without boundary,
coming for my body & soul; a bloodthirsty demon.

I died the day I saw a sheep,
wearing that immaculate drapery,
its face lit up in innocence—
an attraction for hope built like a castle.

But it wasn't a sheep I saw,
I saw a wolf, dressed like
a harmless sheep
stalking me like a prey.
I came & it ate my flesh & drank my blood,
leaving my bones on the street of disappointment.

I saw my beloved smiling at me
yet, at the chime of the high hour,
he did me like Judas,
& our world turned,
from light to darkness,
from love to hatred,
from smiles to frowns,
from laughter to cries,
from celebration to mourning.

Hope lost & trust shattered
for greed crept in & life became a battlefield.
That was the day I died.

Greed held the blade
tearing it into the depth of my tummy
what death can I die again
when each memory
Is a deeper thrust
of yesterday's blade?
Tell me! What death is it
to die again?
For I have died so many deaths from the deep wounds
of betrayal . . .

Hannie Rouweler (June 13, 1951, Goor, Netherlands) is a poet, translator, and an editor of various international poetry collections. Her sources of inspiration are nature, love, loss, childhood memories and travel. She has authored 40 poetry volumes, including translations in several foreign languages. Her poems have been translated into about 30 languages.

Hij stond aan de deur
Hannie Rouweler

Ik zag hem langs het raam. Hij zocht een weg
maar haperde bij de konijnen. Verborgen
in hokken als het stormt met weer en wind.

Ik kon naar buiten lopen. Ik bleef binnen
slot van de deur af. Een achterdeur
blijft niet voor iedereen meer open staan.

Zoals vroeger: herken je die tijd dat ieder
langs ramen liep en zo naar binnen ging?
Je rook koffie en appeltaart vanaf de straat.

Als een man hier naar binnen loopt. Hij loopt langs
schilderijen, boeken, stapels papier, kussens.
Er is geen ander pad over een ander vloerkleed.

He Was at the Door
Hannie Rouweler

I saw him past the window. He looked for a way
but faltered with the rabbits. Hidden
in lofts when it storms with wind and weather.

I could walk out. I stayed indoors
lock off the door. A back door
is no longer open to everyone.

Like before: do you recognize times that everyone
walked past windows and went in just like that?
You smelled coffee and apple pie from the street.

If a man walks into my house. He is walking
past paintings, books, piles of paper, cushions.
There is no other path across another rug.

Born in Dhaka, Bangladesh, Rubab Abdullah is now a citizen of the United States. She is a published poet whose work has appeared in various prestigious international anthologies and e-zines, including Spillwords Press, Columbus Free Press, Rose Books (in affiliation with Ave U Publisher), and Inner Child Press International.

Knowing the Self
Rubab Abdullah

Part I
(Insatiable)

In swirls of wind-storm
I have an unyielding faith
My fate may be twisted
But my reveries live.

Amidst the bustling town
You hear voluble me,
Your adoration vibrates my being
Like the Sun proclaiming light's glory.

Withered with years
All my laughs and tears,
My inked words too
Become my voice.

Part II
(Know us)

My pursuit to discern ourselves
Shall never come to a close,
My dealings with you
Shall only spread
Over endless days and nights.

To see the frozen shut window
My heart sobs for freedom,
Watching the rainbow forming
Deep in my heart
I am as enthralled as you are.

Poetry... The Best of 2020

In the endless disruptions
We become,
Nature harbors recluses like us --
Platonic lovers on a spiritual journey.

Khalid Imam is the Founder/Curator of All Poets Network. He has participated in the 2017 Wole Soyinka Foundation/SAIL Program in Lebanon. He is a teacher, translator and multiple award-winning bilingual playwright and poet, and has published in the UK, the U.S.A., India, Germany, Canada and Poland.

I Am . . .
Khalid Imam

I am a hummingbird
I fly forward and backward.

Like a fish,
I am so flexible.
I can fly sideways
I can dive
I can soar
I can harbor on a spot.

Sometimes,
I am like an ostrich
Running with the speed
Faster than Bolt.

I am a camel,
I endure long distance walks,
I can withstand thirst
And long desert journeys
For weeks without food.

Who I am or what I am
Is a mystery to many
Because I am me.

D. L. Davis holds 3rd Place in the 2010 San Diego Poetry Slam; hosts the internet poetry radio show, Xpressions Radio – Bad Boys Kitchen, and is the 2010 National Poetry Award Winner. He has a poetry book *My Soul Told Me To* (2019) and *SHORTS* (2020), a poetry CD to his credit.

dldavisthepoet (IG / FB / TWITTER)
dldavisthepoet.com

Who Am I?
D. L. Davis The Poet

I am a ghetto bastard born in the heart of LA, Lost Angels
Raised in alleyways, streets devoid of hope with dim lights
so it was hard to see the future

The Concrete Jungle. At the crossroads of Chaos and Disorder.
Where I learned a few tricks, saw chicks turn a few tricks and
shallow holes swallow chocolate bodies whole. The stage was set.
The scene isn't pretty, but everyone knew their role

I am Martin's dream, deferred but not given up on
I come from a family of coke lines to writing dope lines and I love the high. I
am anger and resentment.
I am the raging beast who is calmed by the music of my wife's voice when she speaks
She reminds me life is not always black and white
Life, is a rainbow in a bag, Trayvon
It's, 50 shades of Gray; Freddie
There's various hues and beauty in the blues, especially when a lady sings it

I am mean muggin' with a cold stone exterior
But I turn gooey like putty when I hear grandpa and daddy
I am the son who speaks silently in codes only my wife can decipher
I am lyrics that married melodies and gave birth to hope in a manger for all to adore

I am priceless
Abstract and a bit complex, but you saw thru all my flaws and put a ring on it
Now I know my worth
I'm cool as Morris Day. Smooth as a Botti sax on a jazz track. I'm woke!

I know, skin is the biggest organ, but my melanin makes it a sin-sssation. I am,
a Georgia road from Ahmaud Arbery. A
Texas lane from Sandra Bland and

a Staten Island street from Eric Garner
This quarantine is not new to me. Hell! I've been scared to go somewhere for fear of dying for almost 50 yrs.

And I am still here

That has got to count for something

Jaydeep Sarangi is a poet, translator, an academic and interviewer, who is involved in the poetry movement. He is a widely anthologized and reviewed bilingual poet with eight collections in English to his credit. He is Vice President of GIEWEC and Vice President of the Executive Council, IPPL, and ICCR (Kolkata).

jaydeepsarangi@gmail.com

Love
Jaydeep Sarangi

All along the rainy earth
a wild game of hearts is played
at all our ears and eyes
for a result
that is never complete.

And then a whisper, a rush

I can hear a line
travel back through the bird-cries.
This last, long night of waiting
promises to find her for the first time.

From Patra, Greece, Eftichia Kapardeli has a doctorate from the Arts and Culture World Academy. She writes poetry, short stories, haiku, and essays, and has several national awards. She studied journalism in A.K.E.M. Her poems appeared in numerous national and international anthologies. She has membership with World Poets' Society, IWA, and Poetas del Mundo.

Γενεθλια Γη
Eftichia Kapardeli

Έζησα σε ένα ατελείωτο
χωρισμό δακρύων
πάντα περιπλανιόμουν στην μεγάλη
ευτυχία των ρόδων
στους ώμους μου ατελείωτα
μικρά ουράνια τόξα
στην μέση του απείρου
των άστρων οι ανάσες
τρυπούσαν την καρδιά μου

Έζησα με ανοιχτά παράθυρα
Στις αποχρώσεις των χρόνων
Και εκείνη την μοναδική ώρα
σε έναν νέο Αιώνα δραπέτευσα

Διέσχισα τους μεγάλους δρόμους
Ντυμένη την ελαφριά περπατησιά
των παιδικών μου χρόνων

Ω! πόσο γλυκαίνει η καρδιά
Χέρια τρυφερά ,χείλη απαλά
Στην γενέθλια γη
των πρώτων ρόδων
Χρυσές πεταλούδες θριάμβου
Ελεύθερες το πλούσιο φως μοιράζουν

On Birthday Land
Eftichia Kapardeli

I lived in an endless
separation of tears
I always wandering
in the big happiness of roses
on my shoulders endlessly
rainbows small
in the infinity of middle
the breaths of the Stars
pierced my heart

I lived with windows open
In shades of years
And at that unique time
in a new Century I escaped

I crossed the big roads
Dressed in light walking
of my childhood

Oh! how sweet the heart is
Hands tender, lips gently
On birthday land
of the first roses
Free the rich light of sharing
golden triumph butterflies

Poets of the World

Nigar Arif was born in 1993 in Azerbaijan. She studied in the English Department at Azerbaijan State Pedagogical University. She is a member of the World Youth Turkish Writers' Union and the International Forum for Creativity and Humanity in Morocco. Her poems have been translated into different languages and published in various countries.

Humans' Rain
Nigar Arif

Here is the city,
people break out and leave . . .
Here are the snows and rains,
washing their footprints . . .
Even the sun shines in every morning,
Winds blow and sleek
Nothing can remove those,
Nothing can be changed . . .
People soak up to its memory
from its pocky face.
They fetch their colors with themselves
keeping the city pale.
Everywhere is dull,
Everything turns to a grey tale.
People rain and rain falls from their eyes
in every single day
And those getting wet in the heart of this city
who can't run away
Humans are raining cats and dogs,
Ambulances revolve like the umbrellas
under the sick drops . . .
Either the nights or the noons
wobble from their homes.
The whole world tumble from its place
and falls . . .
Day by day, week by week
Streets become empty
The roads, cafes see the end.
The shoulders of the heavy shops
are going to bend . . .
The huge buildings, the small houses
between the city's arms
peeping out with fear at the naked depth
that idles in the villages, travels to the countries
Lonely trees are getting bored
The flowers, birds and meadows

from the dusty feet of this city
missing of the man
Who knows?
May be in their own languages
they even rail
this damn, teasing quarantine.
Now we know, mom
Cities and countries
can also catch the diseases . . .
What can i say?
Don't worry,
everything will be okay.
There are hopes
that draw out till the hair of this city . . .
There are our dreams putting the hands to its forehead
to check the heat . . .
May be we found the best treatment, mom,
Love is the best engraftment
as you always said . . .

Miled Khaldi, 39, is a teacher of English and a writer from Tunisia. He has two books to his credit, *Lithium Visions and Platinum Sprouts* and *The Code of Jahbazed*. He is passionate about travelling, reading, and contemplation.

miledkhaldi@yahoo.fr

The Boomerang
Miled Khaldi

I've picked from the rubble a walking-stick,
That walks at dawn the trembling streets.
Don't tread ash over the Persian carpet,
For the pores run over with our corpses.
The fret is not a reliable sword yet it doesn't
Intend to creep into another rhythm, into
Another battlefield.
Olive branches blush, don't feign unscientific espionage.
Refresh those who have elephantine memories.
Léthé leaps skywards, drowns my bitter-sweet
Seconds. I forget, make me forget what will happen on
The prospect,
Our relics of glory and passion blossom into the Eden
Of homeland.
Hold on! We need Indira, we do need something alike.
Let's depart, providence is flaking off slowly but surely . . .
Providence trails away to a pleasing collapse, trails away
To a divided human whole . . .
Palestinian epic awaits long-held peace, long-held leap.
Don't trust your upturn, nor the gentle lines,
The ladder is snow-made, seasoned with the rubble of
Babylon . . .
How lash to breakfast at midnight on Venus cake
And vernal rain!!
The gipsy foreteller, as yet unborn confided in me
The coming years would bring rebel comets, would bring
A full sky of olive trees . . .
Pseudo is your entity; what lies above me flutters
Underfoot.
Free the cage, let the wired structure twitter, compose
The tenth symphony . . .
Splendid is the jumble, raise it to your head,
Knead the dough into open vistas of a recognized dignity.
The civilization of nose wrinkles lavender in disgust
When civilians are bereft of crying shoulders.
  I'm brimming over with Arabia from . . . Zanoubia . . .

To Carthage.
No one dares their faults, their achievements, their
Musk roses.
We seek no compliments to ease the rather
Bruised Ego, no adversaries to show them our sales.
I'll fling in two hours the sun with a boomerang;
The former will get back; the latter will get lost.
It will turn into a culture of steam and seam.
Nothing returns but if . . .
Go surfing on the wrinkles in your age-like face.
The surf turns to a resilient swell, rather to local
Languages out of the embryonic globalization . . .
Relish your time, all is yours . . . the crumple will
Straighten up twice a smile . . . twice a nod . . .

Linda Imbler is the author of five paperback poetry collections and three e-book collections (Soma Publishing.) She lives in Wichita, Kansas with her husband, Mike the Luthier, several quite intelligent saltwater fish, and an ever-growing family of gorgeous guitars.

lindaspoetryblog.blogspot.com.

Crystal Ships
Linda Imbler

The sea splatters its foam
like pearls for which divers dive.
Salt that could rust ships
gives life, under the waters blue.
Living creatures act as fathomable archangels
above the bones of crystal ships.
And all are protected by God.

Babatunde Waliyullah Adesokan (Toonday) is from Oyo State, Nigeria. He works with Firstbank of Nigeria. An OAU graduate, he is a lover of poetry; a lover of everything that breathes.

Juliet's Letter & Romeo's Response
Babatunde Waliyullah Adesokan

Juliet's Letter
Romeo, take me where we would be alone,
where the world could end at the instance
it starts, where bodies could suffer its quake
& emotions erupt, where questions are
declaratives & need no answers.

Romeo, touch all my forgotten follicles, abduct
me till pleasure could garnish me with stars &
moons beneath the roof of my closed eyelids,
touch me till you awake the dead seeds in me,
spurting lives & newness.

Romeo, be the arrow, the quiver, the hunter,
I'd be the game. shoot at me. hunt me. I am
 the game. end this war with a quavering pleasure.
pour in me a rain of delight. viscous with lives
that could walk the seeds to a continuation of
us. Oh, Romeo!
………………………………………
Romeo's Response
Oh Juliet!
Be calm. Emotions can be a tumultuous sea
that swallows any ship of entanglement.
Rather, let me tend you with crafty care.
Feel out every strand of your delicate parts.
Let me sail our ship through this devouring
passion, un-capsized. I hold the rudder while
we drift in a glee that moderates the fiery craving.

Oh Juliet!
Be my after-rain. Fill me with green smell
of fertility. Fill me with your clear, crispy
skin that opens like the sky after a proper
downpour. Fill me with newness that fore-
tells hope after a deluge that clears the

cloudy part of our minds. Kill me softly with
indulgence that reignites the exuberance
we eschew. For me, yield again & again until
this ship, after a lengthy sojourn, finally
capsizes into you. I am yours, oh Juliet.

Lucky Stephen Onyah, a Lagosian by birth, is a Mathematics teacher and Principal at Genii Field College and an English teacher with the World English Institute. He is a poet, an entrepreneur and a public speaker.

Pen Versus Sword
Lucky Stephen Onyah

"A pen is mightier than a sword".
A thought considered as absurd.
True power doesn't come via coercion.
But in the fine arts of written persuasion.

Men may fear one with a fierce sword.
Still defies it, but yields to penned accord.
The sword may be born from fiery flame.
Yet have lost great wars via the quill's fame.

If inspired wordsmith harnesses pen's might.
It restrain swordsmiths from every fight.
Sacred text in ages have tamed war lords.
Yet has raised sages and birthed pen lords.

The sword have been shamed for taking lives.
The bleeding pen do rejoice for saving lives.
"Seek peace and pursue it", says scripture.
Gracious words written to secure your future.

Padmaja Iyengar-Paddy's maiden poetry collection, *P-En-Chants* was recognized by the India Book of Records. The recipient of several awards, Paddy has compiled and edited 6 international multilingual poetry anthologies with *Amaravati Poetic Prism* between 2016 to 2019. This publication was distinguished by Coca-Cola India's Limca Book of Records as the "Poetry Anthology in Most Languages".

When . . .
Padmaja Iyengar-Paddy

When you feel totally down and out
Beset by nagging worries and doubt
Go watch some comedy shows
Let out some ha-ha and ho-hos
And see a smile replacing the pout

When everything around seems to irk
And mind absolutely refuses to work
Try cooking a new dish
Veg, non-veg or some fish
And see your creation bring on a smirk

When creativity is at an ebb low
And ideation seems on a go-slow
Try doing a translation
As a means of diversion
And you will soon get into the flow

When unrequited love refuses to die
And mind questions: why, why, why
Go out and let your hair down
Use red hue to paint the town
And soon you'll find your spirits high

When for an issue you find no solution
And mind seems beset with confusion
Use an effective mental tissue
To wipe the mind off the issue
And soon, the issue will find resolution

Rini Valentina is a writer from Indonesia who has written several books of poetry and short stories and has published five international anthology books in English, Spanish and Indonesian since 2017.

Hallucinating Clouds
Rini Valentina

Cloud asked the moon
Why are the stars so far away?
Never want to come down!
Laughing with us . . .
Or for a moment play together
Releasing the happiness
Paint stories
Just forgetting the pinch hurts
Just forgetting the spirit that Narendra's steps went through
Oh . . . who is he?
Is it a man?
Suddenly she asked to her body
A man with a club as big as his calf
Or just an ordinary man?
With a secret style behind the sunscreen?
Ahh . . . I hope it's not a gallon of cream
skin armor that cringes dark color
Hopefully just guessing
Just guessing . . .
Because patience is tired of keeping
Because patient is tired of acting as a cinema-style body guard
Ahh . . . never mind . . .
Cloud finally gave up
Shame to ask the moon again
After all, there was never an answer . . .

Ashok K. Bhargava is a poet and public speaker. He has five books of poetry to his credit. He is president of Writers International Network of Canada.

Absolutely
Ashok Bhargava

folded hands
hold silence
in the dark

spirit
oscillate
from eternity to infinity

my body
a fragile glass
can shatter easily

my resolve
stronger than steel
unbreakable

look anywhere
for me
find me there

Don't wait
for an approximation
I am it
you are it
we are it

Christena AV Williams is a Jamaican poet, multiple award-winning author, youth volunteer, self-publisher, historian, and philosopher. She originates from Portmore, St. Catherine. She has authored *Pearls Among Stones* that awarded her the Prime Minister's National Youth prize. P.O.E.T. has awarded her with the 2020 International Spoken Word Artist prize.

Tomboy
Christena AV Williams

From I was growing up, neighbours would jokingly called me Tomboy
I understood to a degree what it meant at age ten
But it was not until I was twenty-five, I despise its connotations
I had accepted my femininity
But their roles of how I should speak and act
Their condescending laws, values, morals, ethic and standards
I naturally forbade.

I did not accept Tom because it was masculine
I did not accept Tom as I was no peeping Tom or Uncle Tom
Boy was not my Ideal
Not Idea
Not my gender
I was female and a girl who did not fit their stereotype.

I guess I have always been a rebel
A revolutionist
Not standard or a carbon copy
Was not dolly faced lipstick glossy fake
I made people uneasy when I spoke
My presence was felt without even an exhale
Their constant bickering to act girl, dress girl and be girl
As it was their way of reminding me that I should know my place.

My feminine energy was so strong that other women despised me
Men got attracted while others discombobulated with their own insecurities
I was a trigger to their questions
I surely made a mark.

It is not easy for anyone to love and accept me
It is not easy because I am a walking tabloid that people gossip about
As their lips are like opium
My fate was in the hands of the people
Oh, they hated me.

I was epitome of female freedom to a degree
I wore comfort
Grace with strength
Even in my fragile state
Even when my womanliness I could not hide
Because of tenderness of the heart
I was steadfast with a calculated mind that never stopped unwinding
Only the brave could commit to me.

My voice was one point my hatred now it is my uniqueness
There were times, a few moments that I felt ashamed of my body,
My nature, my clothes
Was a woman so incapable of greatness that they had to be a Tomboy?
Who was Tom this phantom and why was I in comparison
My femininity was in questioned
Never my masculinity.

Poets of the World

The cathartic word brings healing for both the author and her audience. Kay Salady is a Washingtonian who has contributed to numerous publications that aim toward global peace. Her objective is instilling the simple truth that during the times in our lives when we thought we were alone, someone else was there.

His Invitation
Kay Salady

I fell in love with the distance
An arm's length away
Yet impossible to hold
I reached out to grasp
His invitation
Then searched the world for him
As he inhaled
The supplication of a child
Who hungered every instant
That led me to believe
That he was waiting
A hint of his divinity
Fed fire to the flame
That burned inside my chest
And I cried out for reprieve
Sealing away my tears
Inside his alabaster jars
Perhaps tonight he'll come
To accept my offering
I will behold his dazzling eyes
And I will fully realize
A life well-lived

Dr. Thirupurasundari C J (Dazzle), holds a doctorate and a gold medal in Life Sciences. She has publications in peer-reviewed journals, and possesses research experience in cancer, diabetes and horticulture. In addition to being an artist, a poet, freelancer, and an editor for an e-zine, she draws inspiration from others and is always cheerful.

My Mind's Eyes
Thirupurasundari CJ

Birthdays, anniversaries, festivals,
Our blessings, fixed!
Reunions, trips, adventure programs,
Captured on celluloid,
As I flip through the photo album,
Treasuring life time memories.

Members of my extended family,
Few sneaked peeks in stills,
Few posed for candid shots,
Few with slouched postures,
Weird looks, squinty eyes,
Crazy angels, eccentric moustaches,
Diverse fashion unveiled, each distinctive,
Amidst vibrant colours,
Capturing the essence of disarrayed happiness,
Eternal sparkles with my relations!

A sweet voyage through the time,
First steps of my niece and nephew,
Their euphoric expressions,
Disheveled hair or tonsured heads,
Still getting the whiff of those sandal pastes,
Funny dress patters, interesting props,
Adoringly imprinted in my mind,
I wear a gleaming face,
Incredible impressions!

Bizarre moments with friends,
Unconditional love of parents and siblings,
Our ecstatic countenances,
Black and white freeze- snaps of grandparents,
Our legacy made to last,
Splashing reminiscings,
Inestimable belongings!

Love and togetherness,
Life made worthwhile,
Both complementing each other,
Secured images with my partner,
Stitched with intimacy,
Held fast with care and endearment,
Append boundless emotional touch to my photo book,
All the merry!

Optical illusions, bright locations,
Fantastical forced perspective photographs,
Technology upgradations,
Spell bounding though!

Svelte soft cover or classic hard covers,
Whatever, matte or glossy stills,
Aesthetic layouts, gorgeous frames,
My albums are truly a comforter,
Explicit memoirs,
Making my hippocampus and amygdala of my brain,
Work unblemished.

My albums, an out and out material,
To relive my moments!

Ratan Ghosh, (PhD), is an Indian poet, editor, freelancer, short story writer, and above all, a teacher and a researcher. His poems have been featured in many international E- journals, print journals and anthologies across the globe. He has authored *My Love*, *Gender Disparity*, *Sunup*, *Cascade*, and *The Talisman and Other Tales*.

Dead City
Ratan Ghosh

Corpses, cries and woes . . .
Rolling and rolling in the dusty roads
Nameless faces, throats and bodies
Enfolded and heaped among the ghostly lobbies
Doctors, Nurses and Cops . . .
I see them afraid of being sympathetic to their jobs
Thrusting, thrusting and thrusting all the lifeless destitute
Relatives and country men began weeping while saw this heartless news
Rolling, rolling and rolling tears fell upon their cheeks
As the dead city lost to feel the minimum human needs
Walking all alone I see the kingdom of Hades
Where infernal powers ruling over the innocent corpses and beds
How long this deadly kingdom will rule over justice and peace?
My heart woes seeing the dances of inhuman beasts

Born in Guelma, Algeria, Warda Zerguine is a poet, writer and journalist. She wrote and recited poems in Arabic, French and English. She has participated in different international anthologies in Serbia, Tunisia, the USA, Indonesia , India, and Algeria. Some of her poems have been translated into Ouzbek, Serbian, Spanish and Italian.

Be My Love
Warda Zerguine

In your eyes I see myself
In your tears I drown
I want you to be
Near me . . .
Your forgiveness i owe you
Your love i need
May your heart receive me . . .
Like a king and a queen
I want you to believe me . . .
I want you to see me . . .
So get ready
It's my right
Oh how much i love your voice
And your laugh.. oh my faith
I will not know why
Only you my heart.

Hassan Hegazy Hassan is a poet and translator from Egypt. He has a B.A. from Zagazig University in Arts and Education with an English major. A member of the Egyptian Writers Union, the Egyptian Translators and Linguists Association, and the Arab Internet Writers Union, he has authored several books on poetry and translation.

If Only I Had
Hassan Hegazy Hassan

If only I had two wings

like a bird,

If only I had perfume

like Anemones,

If I had Honey

like the fruits of Pomegranate,

If only I had Power

Like King Solomon,

If only I owned the world

Or I own the Garden of Redwan:

I would have put all the women

in one scale and put you in the other

and my heart is with you

Your scale would be heavier

So, say what you want

and boast as you wish

Your name will immortalize

in my poetry over time!

لو كان لي
حسن حجازي حسن
مصر
///
لو كان لي كالطير جناحان ,
لو كانَ لي عطرٌ كشقائق النعمان ,
لو كان لي شهدٌ كحبِ الرمان ,
لو كانَ لي مُلكٌ كمُلك سليمان ,
لو كنتُ أملكُ العالم وحدي
أو أملكُ جنة رضوان :
لوضعتُ نساءَ العالم
في كفة
ووضعتكِ في كفة
وقلبي معك
لرجحت كفتكِ بالميزان !
فقولي ما شئت
وتيهي على العالمِ
كما شئتِ
فسيخلدُ اسمكِ
في شعري
على مر الأزمان !
///

Iram Fatima 'Ashi', a nonresident Indian who lives in Saudi Arabia, is a poet, writer, painter, and overall, an artist by heart. Her work has appeared in more than 50 anthologies and she has won 3 awards from Aagman for her literary contributions.

The Traveler
Iram Fatima 'Ashi'

I am a traveler, started my journey since I was born,
I am desirous to explore the whole world and universe,
All deep depths, darkness and highness of the heights,
I want to travel to discover all the fascinating horizons.

I had reached the peaks of the mountains,
To feel like a king who sees everything from heights,
Tiny small helpless creatures are visible from there,
But a view to valley horrified me by the fear of fall.

I went to the sea to play with sea waves,
To float carefree in the depth of the sea,
To discover beauty to collect pearls for me,
Being lost in the deep dark sea again horrified me.

I explored dense vegetation dominated by trees,
Deep, dark, silent, lonesome and horrifying jungles,
Only breeze and bird's chirping was breaking the silence,
The wildness of that mystified and triggered my inner fears.

At this moment I realized, I have to change my path,
Outer universe to deep inside my self,
To fight with my insecurities and fears,
The world is beautiful if I travel inside my soul.

Poets of the World

Eden Soriano Trinidad hails from the Philippines. The University of the Philippines Institute of Creative Writing published five of her books. Her poems have been featured on the full page of *Haiphong Weekend*, *Văn Nghệ, Nhật Lệ Vietnam* – a literary magazine, and *China Science Herald*. She translated *Ithaca Poems* into Filipino.

Mt. Pinatubo
Eden Soriano Trinidad

A great man from Zambales Philippines
Once hid and fought the guerillas in this mountain.

In (March 17) 1957, "Mt. Pinatubo" Presidential plane
Crashed and ended the life of Ramon Magsaysay Sr.
Beloved President of the Philippines

Indeed, a great man from Iba, Zambales
Met his tragic end
In the lonely mountainside
Together with his friends.

How his life ended was written
For one survived to defend
He wrote a book and told the story of his dreadful end.
Which no one will know if not for a dear friend.

In 1991, "Mt Pinatubo" the volcano then
It indeed ended hundreds of lives and living
Of people in our dear province
Turning a state of deep misery in every being.

The skies turned dark heavens turned mad;
Fierce spewed greatly
Seemed God was asleep unmindful of
Hovering death and volcanic fury.

Today, "Mt. Pinatubo" stood
In his impressive, gigantic crater sea
Teasing every soul to find solace
Making you forget it was then very deadly.

Yvette Murrell, Power, Voice & Choice Coach, has multifaceted cross-sector accomplishments in business, education and expressive arts. She is enjoying full-bellied laughter and dreaming a life sweet beyond her imagination! She revels in the following identities: twin, mother, facilitator, artist, writer and alchemist.

http://yvettemurrell.com/ IG:@divineguidanceangel

Bridges
Yvette Murrell

Joy can only go so far when you won't hold pain.
Life can only go so far when you won't hold death.
Shared humanity is about holding both with love and integrity.
This is a challenging place to stand and a powerful place to be.

Recognize how the past is useful to bring love to the present.
Recognize how dreaming is useful to generate the future.
Recognize how understanding lives in relevant metaphors.
Recognize the work generated by painful experiences.
Recognize the opportunity to love, accept, forgive and cherish all.
Recognize the invitation to be authentic, feel and be with what is.
Recognize the choice to be present and hold meaningful boundaries.
Recognize when you are free, someone is holding the container in which you are twirling.
Recognize where you are listening from.
Recognize where you are observing from.
Recognize where you are now.
If you have it, build the bridge to connect with others. If not,
    welcome them on the journey. If they choose not to build the bridge to the part
    of themselves that is reflected in you, then remember when you were there
    and give them permission not to connect. Give them permission to be in separation
    and bless them with love for their journey. Then weep for the pain of separation
    and let the tears become rivers, let rivers become oceans and let mother earth
    spew her lava blood into the ocean, building new island bridges of her own.

Poets of the World

Semih Bilgiç is a Turkish teacher and a poet. His poems, which address humanity, are about life. He considers the world as only a dream.

Your Story
Semih Bilgiç

if you are watching a cloud
look at your shadow on the ground
your life is as long as your dreams
nightmares are tramps

your story is not the same
hearts are far apart

Poets of the World

Somasuntharampillai Pathmanthan has 3 volumes of his own poetry and 3 collections of poems in translation to his credit. His work appeared in prestigious journals abroad. 'Sopa', as he is popularly known in literary circles, has presented papers in many international fora, including SAARC Literature Festivals (Delhi) and Poets Translating Poets (Frankfurt).

An Ode to a Toad
Somasuntharampillai Pathmanathan ('Sopa')

A warm June morning
I was enjoying a bath
It was then I saw him
staring at me innocently
ensconced on the edge
of the bath–tub

Wet, brown and shiny
Honestly at first sight
I didn't like him
Instinctively
I felt like
sweeping him away
But how?
I didn't want to touch him
Eyes glistening
he looked sticky,
I was getting late
Having finished my bath
I left hurriedly
leaving him

The following morning too
He was there
Quite a nuisance
I thought
Splashed on him a bucketful
of warm water
He seemed to enjoy it!

The encounter continued
every morning
neither party giving in

Poets of the World

I was becoming philosophical
"Why do I harbor
An unreasonable abhorrence
for the visitor?
has he no right
To share my bathroom?
Are my pronouncements
'let all living beings on earth be happy!"
Bogus and hollow?

I could feel
a transformation
Coming over me
Avoidance gave way
to expectation
Disgust to admiration

It was a holiday
As I entered, relaxed
I couldn't believe my eyes!
My visitor was
there as usual
He had brought a partner
A dainty slim dame!
'Oh, no!' I cried
You both would bring forth
A litter of tadpoles
And oust me
from my bathroom
'tampattam tampattam!'
croaked the dainty dame
'Seeking asylum?'
'tampattam, tampattam!'
"Ok" I relented
"But be careful!
A rattlesnake

frequents our garden!"
My mind is at ease
When monsoon commences
next month
I will go to sleep
lulled by the cacophony
"tampattam, tampattam"
Not a bad prospect, is it?

Laura Fitzgerald, a mother of three, lives in Ballina, Co. Tipperary. She has recently reignited her passion to write poems and has contributed to Aulos: *An Anthology of English Poetry*, Soflay Inc. Literary Website, *Caravan: Monsoon and Travel Narratives* – literary engagements that afforded her the confidence to share her poetry further.

Broken Porcelain Faces
Laura Fitzgerald

A child sits upon a bed and gazes
at her mother's peculiar collection
of circus clowns with porcelain faces.
Each one carefully selected and meticulously
placed on rickety shelves, adorning the wall.
A kaleidoscope of every color
that stretches across the rainbow.
As the sun streams through the
nylon curtains, illuminating the various
painted expressions each one exhibits.
Neither they nor she are privy to
the fate that would befall them.
For the pallid walls that they embellish,
hold secrets never uttered aloud,
Until this fateful night.
At ungodly hour, the walls did shake,
A symposium of venomous tongues
as two who made such holy vows,
reign unholy fists upon each other.
As innocent babes lie sleeping
within a parent's volatile warzone.
Contemptible barrage of insults and acrimony,
A hateful tempo builds to a rising crescendo
Of a dysfunctional matrimony,
Crashing sounds of objects breaking.
Broken hearts,
Broken bonds,
broken promises and . . .
broken faces.
Porcelain faces,
as proud circus clowns perform a spectacular final act.
As night gives way and surrenders
to the barging misty morning light,

The child wanders into the aftereffects
of a long night's battle, where no-one won.
At her feet, the scattered pieces of the
familiar faces she had once admired with wonder.
No longer rows of pristine beauty,
Now, a multitude of unrecognizable parts,
dappled with an extra scarlet color
which had not been present before.
A mistimed step amongst the carnage
offers a small cut to the side of her foot.
She winces, as fresh, red blood begins
to slowly ooze from the open wound.
Yet strangely, she feels no pain.
For next to what her eyes and ears have
witnessed, it is as soft as a feathered kiss.
glancing down to her bare feet as
the jagged shells of what once was,
were now no more, nothing but dust and chaos.
Amid this smoking battlefield lies two
comatose bodies flaccidly entangled,
Breathing in opaque air replenishing their lungs
Keeping their selfish hearts beating.
Hearts that should know better.
Exhaling all lucid memory and accountability,
with alcohol fumes and silent regret.
The child turns the key to sibling's doors,
for fear of more cuts to the innocent
barefoot wanderer, should they awaken.
She fetches a broom and heavy plastic
bags and sweeps away all trace of conflict.
Each fragmented casualty of war gathered
and banished to darkness forever.
She would never again lay eyes upon
their psychedelic colors in rows of six.
Nor study each outlined smile or frown.
The shining faces of the stereotypically

jovial figures would sparkle no more.
Silken outfits trimmed with lace that
took her to a magical place for a time.
Instead, they shall forever exist in black.
The rickety shelves, now empty, a reminder
of what lies behind a carefully etched smile.
For now, the house is silent and calm,
In the wake of bitter discourse and harm.
Swords left lying in the dirt, surrounding
two wounded soldiers deep in capitulation.
No remorse nor earnest excuse,
Until the next hostile engagement ensues.

Poets of the World

Nket-Awaji Alpheaus is a poet, critic and an essayist. He writes from Rivers State.

The Casualties
Nket-Awaji Alpheaus

The casualties are not only those
Who are votary for intermittent interment;
The seedlike heads we plant
In the world's farm and harvest memory.

The casualties are those of us
Bearing the blotched lines of life,
Who must bear the ghouls of memories
Reeked of the incense of earth.

The casualties of this war,
Where the paths to our bowels
Are the battlefield - your foe invisible . . .
Are the indigent of this patched earth.

The casualties are wodge of tongues
Dallying for politrick palling palliative,
Who must learn how to scoop sand
For a mirage meal from power bowl.

The casualties are the scaled brains
Whose minds are fish trapped in a net
And hooked with business bait;
Or cloying victim fish to a net.

This wind blows in a pall of cloud,
And rears more kleptomaniac claws.
The casualties are the late mourners
Thrusted with the arrears of morning.

Here we are schooled in death:
While others choke out of breath,
Others are skeined in death . . .
And we are all casualties of the war.

But we - out of sleep but full of dreams -
Must sing our brothers good bedtime songs:
"Sleep jolly in God's right breast"
For they cannot emulsify with us.

Poetry... The Best of 2020

Nataša Sardžoska (1979, Skopje) – poet, writer, polyglot translator, anthropologist, has authored poetry books, short stories, essays, literary translations, and columns. Some of her poems appeared in distinguished literary journals worldwide. She attends international poetry festivals, performing, among others, in the Academy of Arts in Berlin and in the Yaffa Theatre in Tel Aviv.

The Echo of Silence
Nataša Sardžoska

I do not ask you why because there is
nothing to be asked. I do not know the reason
of these letters. there is only a faint reminiscence left. a scent of the profane
memory remained. but I know how to sing the vestiges of the indignant.
I know how this happens. I know how the shadow falls
over the curtain of your white nights behind your words
and how you forget the light the indelible trembling
the mute joy in the throat. and I know how your response
is drowning in the wandering echo of your silence.
I know. I know how that happens. I know how you kill your heart
first before even killing me inside of it.

Brindha Vinodh is an Indian currently residing in the United States of America. She is a postgraduate in Econometrics but a writer within. She has been widely published in the international arena through journals, e-zines, online archives and anthologies.

I Will Write, I Will Write
(*A roseate sonnet*)
Brindha Vinodh

I will write, I will write
until this world is a riot
until my funeral flames ignite the torch light.
I will write, I will write
until there are no more tomato hearts to bleed
until war Rests in Peace
until corporate conspiracy stops to breed
until the incessant plunders of earth cease
until the topaz oceans stink no more
until my rhymes break apart into free verses.
Rocks undergo metamorphosis too
Oh! human glacier hearts, will you not melt?
Slumber is a sly serpent, wake up!
Exert yourself, until then I will write!

Ishfaq SaAhil is from Larnoo, Kokernag (state of Jammu and Kashmir), India. He received his early education from English Medium High School in Larnoo. Saahil has an M.A. in English and writes poetry in English and Urdu. His poems have been featured in numerous national and international journals and poetry anthologies.

But!
IshfAq SaAhil

In a new beginning spring
A little pretty boy, with empty shoulders
Through the streets ran.
The sun was rising
Through the mountains and hills,
The beams were sketching the trees on land.

O listen, O innocent child,
Was someone calling,
Don't you know the green hills
And meadows, and pastures green,
And nothing is left in all this, child
Nothing is left in all this
You read, and recite one by one
And do you know
There is freedom of all that boring things,
No, no, no. How could you
And ignore the work of forefathers
And do the prestiges lost,
You don't know, there is nothing
In all this, You want to do,
And there are herds to manage
And sheep, and horse, Candy.
Don't you know that?

If there were books and tales
Of fairies, and songs and poems to sing
As through the broken panes of school
Are heard, and ringing bells
In a balcony; seven and eight a day,
Father! Father!

Boring things, my boy, boring things,
There is nothing as good as Sheeping
And melodies of birds in the hills
And that cold breezes of raining nights,

All is fun in heavy forests: when groves sing,
The winds pass by, in mid sun of a day
When there is summer in hills.

And if there were pallets
To colour the hollow sketches
Of Lions, Tigers and Bears
And a nice pretty parrot
And Crayons of much more colours
And a nice small satchel in my shoulders,
Father! Father!

Terri Lynn Julie Johnson is a first-nations Cree from the Samson Cree Nation in Maskwacis, Alberta, Canada. She was a featured poet in two ICPI anthologies, *A Poetically Spoken Anthology* and in the January 2014 issue of *The Year of the Poet*. Terri has four books to her credit, published by ICPI.

The Bottle
Terri L. Johnson

I found my best friend
and my worst enemy
In the warmth of the bottle.
A relationship so bittersweet.

All days were like pure ecstasy.
Crazy maniacal thoughts swirled.
Thoughts were fuzzy.
Feelings were hugged close.

The liquid kept them inside,
feelings so fierce.
My bottle kept them locked inside
that my mind left them alone.

The bottle was so evil.
It killed me once.
Lifeless and alone.
No more feelings to atone.

But I woke.
My feelings gripped me.
My Savior.
My saving grace.

Without my feelings.
The bottle would have won.
Released were my fate.
Embrace is what I must.

You see my feelings
brought me back.
Waking me for reality.
Making me more woke.

Now I can't turn those
feelings off.
Nor can I lock them away.
They yell for release.

I'm scared to tell.
Scared to feel.
The bottle was my worst enemy
But also my best friend.

Dr. Molly Joseph, a professor, is a poet from Kerala, who writes travelogues, short stories and children books. She has twelve books to her credit, and has won several accolades which include the India Women Achiever's Award 2020. She believes in the power of the word and writes boldly on contemporary matters.

Where Water Sings over the Stones
Molly Joseph

the quick sands
                        of Covid
sweep across,
               shrouding
man's
     survival game . . .

Where are we
        heading to . . .?

You can hear
                       the sand
drifting from
         the tops
and valleys
     throwing back
their despair . . .

it echoes,
               pervades
the near,
               the far,
while pale
            horizons
watch . . .
No, out there
               a plain
awaits . . .

    your abode
of solace . . .

    where water
sings over

        the stones,
the wind
    cools you,
the cattle
    stand in wait
under the trees
       to step down
to the riverside
       to quench
their thirst . . .

wait, wait
    we too must
for
  the sandstorm
to subside
      and the sky
to clear up . . .

Ifeanyi John Nwokeabia is a poet and teacher. He hails from Nibo in Awka South Local Government Area of Anambra State. He has a Nigeria Certificate in Education and a B.A. in Education, both in English Language. He lives in Awka. His work has appeared on different online platforms.

the palm wine tapper
Ifeanyi John Nwokeabia

ears shut to the wailing sky
eyes blinded to the flooding streets
heart hardened and head held straight forward
for nothing stops his movement at mid night

he goes alone amidst the chirping of insects
darkness enveloped his shadowy body
he slithers unnoticed like a snake in a mission
his only light is the lamp tied to his forehead
the lamp is stationed like the moon in the sky

the pathway bushes tug his cloth in compliment
he pulls open the shrubs on his way as a Pathfinder
his bare feet dare the spindle & spine of its pedestal
he sighs away every excruciating prick that prickles
his palms are as soft as bark of trees
his heels naturally break & remain open like ear hole

survival stands straight in success route
he climbs, taps and sells to feed dependent mouths
the height of a palm tree never posed obstacles
he must tap and quench the unquenchable stomachs

Poets of the World

Photo Credit: Dirk Skiba

Eduard Harents (b. 1981), a known poet, lives in Yerevan, Armenia. He is a graduate of the Oriental Studies Department at Yerevan State University. He has authored 10 poem collections. His work appeared in numerous local and international periodicals and anthologies. His poems have been translated into more than 50 languages.

[sic] No Title
Eduard Harents

The color of ink is the fear of ecstasy
with cold landscape of the night,
from its back it was appeared a sudden hand
between innocence and betrayal.

Whose papers the fingerprints are put on? -
with shining after twelve.

The air trembles
like stacked night suit of doubt.

We have to wait
the nudity of dawn . . .

Cross yourself, Bird!

Translated from Armenian by Ani Hakobyan

John Chizoba Vincents . . . the names of three people deliberately seeing through each other; sometimes, at war with each other, at times, as unbreakable ties. They: Them: Us: Representing Boys and their anatomies, Men and their vulnerabilities, and Humans and their imperfections – rosy-track rough and tough roads in-between, living in a lonely room in Lagos, Nigeria.

Lights
John Chizoba Vincent

Last night, we saw god remove this:
blood stained clothes from the sky,
burnt ashes & dust of men of great honour,
he bridled their housed tears almost home
& their memories, he lost in abyss of death.
this is how death guided their hope in tears
& the only pictures seen are restlessness.
Sometimes our bodies melt away from
the salvations of humanity & sacrilegious
spirits & our reflections become scary,
we fold ourselves into brown sorrow like
we'll return here with a sermon of divinity
to redemption, to reconnect those lost in
between fate & destiny & search for freedom.
But
Life is a boring adventure keeping watch
over the tragedies of death & those killed.
every room becomes available for shadows,
black tilted shadows. broken. Teared up.
having the memories & reflections of life,
Bodies burnt by fire, bodies swallowed, bodies
slaughtered; bodies wounded, & those taken.
Journey's full of meanings and mysteries,
feeding its eyes with nightful of uncertainty.
Emeka was engulfed yesterday on auto crash,
His mother planted a forgotten kiss on altars,
Femi was slaughtered by lurking herdsmen,
He never returned from farm & family waited,
Musa admired the sun & was gunned down,
We gather these memories at dawn for Pius
'cause we never know who returns every time.
His deeds will linger from those red flames
raising his names before the lazy clouds to light

up the world from the face of the Earth.
I'm sure god wears him like a paying,
I'm sure he held these lights flags of heroes
closer to him even as he drowned in himself.
Let's these lights keep his memories in our palms
till tomorrow when next we meet.

Asoke Kumar Mitra (b. 1950) hails from Kolkata, India. He has authored two books of poems, *Savage Wind* (bi-lingual; translated into Spanish, with an Italian edition published in Italy) and *Song of Pebbles* (also bi-lingual; translated into French). Poetry, photography, and paintings are his passions.

Rendezvous in the Rain . . .
Asoke Kumar Mitra

(1)

In a moment of joy and sorrow
A spider has come to stay with us, weaving cobwebs
In the core of our hearts

Warm lips of winter
The wind playing with the candle
You are a fantasy
A forgotten melody
Breathless song

Spider is weaving cobwebs
Trapped our hearts
Left skeleton behind

Tonight, twinkling stars and half moon
Invite us for a never before rendezvous
As strangers, as soul mates
No looking behind

Our shadows walked carefully apart . . .

(2)

The wind howls and bangs at my shut door
The rain takes off her yellow raincoat
Her infinite rain-soaked dreamy eyes
Syllables of fear, love and tenderness

Crumpled times, we voyage through
A long night and fatigue,
Swallowed black fugitive clouds
We see an open wound

Our shadows running into the rainy winds.
We rub shoulders, we talk to the edge of silence
The endless circling, madness wrapped in rain
You and I, love fall to dust . . .

(3)

In your eyes me a fugitive rebel
The summer's gone, silence in the air
Tomorrow it's going to rain . . .
Teardrops from the sky

We met as strangers
We looked into each other's eyes
We have shared song of the rain
Melodious rhythm

We raise our arms to the sky
The wild fragrance of rain
Passions swirled in our loneliness
We become stranger again
In our palm only the stain of rain . . .

Alonzo "zO" Gross, a Temple University graduate (English Literature), is a songwriter, dancer, recording artist and writer. He has authored short stories (*Staying Sane* series), two poetry books – *Inspiration, Harmony and the World Within* and *sOuL eLiXiR*, was recognized as Leigh Valley's "Best Spoken Word Poet", and has been featured poet in the film, *VOICES*.

When We Cease All of the Marching . . .
Alonzo Gross

If it were switched,
(Tell me)
How would u feel? /
Would u still bitch,
If for "U" Kaepernick kneeled?/.
What if every day ur people's
Blood would splatter?--
With no regard,
2 ur hard pleas of SCREAMIN'
"WHITE LIVES MATTER!!!"--.
What if?
When u said that,
we laughed more or less/
And said "ALL LIVES MATTER",
Makin A Protest,
2 Yo Protest/
(Oh Yes/) I guarantee,
U would feel it, in yo chest/
The distress/
Of gettin' killed on film
And u gets
no arrest/.
Out of frustration u too,
Would probably riot •
But u"ll never "stomach"
What I say,
it's not in ur "diet" •.
Cuz In ur mind,
u think that Everyone favors u /
Like ur Divine,
Truth is . . .
Yer WHITE PRIVILEGE
ENABLES U /

Poets of the World

I think it's time,
U show empathy,
love and respect ----*
Before there comes a time,
We put more than our foots on yalls necks---.*
Just know I want Peace,
But our gunz is Arching _
So please don't call us Beasts,
When We Cease all of the Marching_.

zO

Pragya Sharma is a poet residing in Muzaffarnagar UP, INDIA. She is an engineering student who has contributed to online prose and poetry magazines a number of times.

The River of life
Pragya Sharma

In the immense sea of lust
be the wave carrying love
In the crowd of masked faces
divulge hidden traces

Among good looks and curves
treasure soul which serves
In a book embracing untrue stories
be the page rich in veracious glories

In depraved court of sinful minds
do justice with pious mankind
In the air of sorrow and lamentation
be someone's breath of delectation

In the dawn of fake promises and lies
hold someone till dusk ever dies
In humongous river of life
Be a fisher catching deepest trench of cries

From Hyderabad, India, Dr. Ashok Chakravarthy Tholana's poems have been published in over 90 countries. His poetry promotes universal brotherhood, peace, protection of environment/nature, and safeguarding children's and human rights. He has received commendations from the former President and Prime Minister (India), Queen Elizabeth (the UK), Princess of Wales, President (France), and the Prime Minister (Switzerland).

tacvarthy@gmail.com

With Themes Upright . . .
Ashok Chakravarthy Tholana

Infiltrated by words, relentlessly
Penetrated by thoughts, endlessly,
The aspiring mind of every poet,
The ever-thirsty pen of every poet,
Expect to impart righteous verses,
Expect to implant themes virtuous.

Pen is mightier than the sword
Can transform the world with words,
With every line in every verse,
Readers across the universe,
Liberated and morally awakened,
To tread a path worth enlightened.

Weaving pleasant words of bliss
Conferring a boon of eternal happiness;
Dousing the fires of hatred and anger,
Let virtuous words make everyone stronger.
Yes, defacing human ignorance and ego,
May every poet's upright themes echo.

From Andhra Pradesh, India, Dr. T. Ramesh Babu is (ad hoc) Assistant Professor of English at JNTUACEP. He is a poet, writer, and soft skills instructor. He has authored 16 international and 2 national papers and has 3 books. Many of his poems have appeared in international anthologies and magazines.

Restless & Defamed Life!
Ramesh Reddy Tera

I too have fantasies, but mine;
Turned into nightmares;
I too crave to have a beautiful life,
But, my destiny led to this hellhole;
My eyes see only two colours;
Black and white; Mostly dark,
Because, I awake nights.
My day kicks off with night;
For me every night as kalaratri;
Men treat me as a sex toy and a puppet;
Irrespective of their age and size
One after another being ready to attack on me;
As wild animals attack on deer;
Moreover they demand for my angelic beauty;
At bargained cost: Ignoring my pain:
They squash my body and blacken;
My reddish skin with cigars and forcible intercourse,
Tormenting unscrupulously for ravishment;
I neither bear the pain nor control the yells;
Yet tears running down as streams;
Still having chuckles on my face.
The white washed walls turned into dark;
With stains as smeared on walls.
Those stains stood as witness of;
My struggles to survive each night;
From wild beasts among four walls.
How long do I bear this pain to feed?
My little children appetite.
Do I have to adjust as it is my fate?
Is it the worth of liberty?
Is it my life?
Don't I have hopeful days ahead as I crave?
O liberty! Are you not for all?

Hussein Habasch is a poet from Afrin, Kurdistan. His poems have been translated into many languages. He has participated in numerous international poetry festivals, including those in Colombia, Nicaragua, France, Puerto Rico, Mexico, Germany, Romania, Lithuania, Morocco, Ecuador, El Salvador, Kosovo, Macedonia, Costa Rica, Slovenia, China, Taiwan, and New York City.

In a Coma
Hussein Habasch

On May 13, 2020, I had an operation to remove a kidney stone. As a result of a medical error during anesthesia, I fell into a complete coma for two consecutive days, and I miraculously survived death. After I left the intensive care unit on the fourth day, I frantically wrote this text in Kurdish, as if I was in a race against time.

In a coma
Your body is not yours
Your mind is not yours
Your brain is not yours
Your soul is not yours
Your being is not yours
Your dreams are not yours
Absolutely nothing is yours!
You are just a vulnerable bird
Stumbling in his flight, like a blind lost his cane
In a fierce war against blindness.

In a coma
You don't know your name nor your title
You don't know your birth date nor your age!
You don't know what time you are in nor what day!
You don't know what month, what season
What year, what century you are in!
Nothing has value in your eternal and vast passivity.

In a coma
You don't feel the time!
No value for the time nor the clockwise
No value for sunrise nor sunset
No value for morning nor night
No value for light nor darkness
No value for fertility nor drought
No value for trees nor flowers
No value for a butterfly's tenderness nor a bird's flutter
No value for the clouds nor the blue sky...
In a coma you are present

And your real presence is your absence
And getting lost in the nothingness abyss
Without limbs nor legs nor strong feet!

In a coma
You forget every day's walking roads
Forget the road to the coffee shop
Forget the road to the bar
Forget the road to the work
Forget the road to the house
Forget your keychain
Forget your keys
Forget your door's lock
Forget your library
Forget the smell of your books
Forget your notebooks and pens
Forget your poems
Forget your daily rituals
Forget your hat
Forget your coat
Forget your shirt
Forget if you are dressed or naked!
No difference, forgetting is the mystery of coma and its blessing.

In a coma
Nothing has value but the Oxygen tube which provide your lungs with air
And to the hoses which feed your body with medicines
And to the anesthetics that sedate the already sedated!
No value but to the adhesive tapes on your chest, which measure your unfelt heartbeats.
No value but to the bed which they threw you in it motionless.
Nothing indicate that you breath.
Nothing indicate that you exist in existence.

In a coma
You won't feel pain even if it's severe
You won't shuffle your breath even if it's a strong rattle
You won't cry even if there is an obligatory reasons to cry
You won't love, and you don't know why you won't?!
You won't cry, and you don't know why you won't?!

No astonishment
No outburst
No amazement…
You look like a statue sculpted from boredom
Or an invisible icon in a ghost church.

In a coma
You like this monkey
Which doesn't see
Doesn't hear
Doesn't talk
And doesn't understand its surroundings
But although
It remains a real being of flesh, blood, and tears.

In a coma
Your eyelid won't flutter
Your cheeks won't blush
Your forehead won't left up
Your eyelashes won't blink
Your heart won't beat
You won't notice the sweat drop on your forehead
You won't wipe the black blood stain from your neck
You just will fade away, your capabilities will vanish and it will become less than ash and lighter than dust.

Coma is a trick
Plot
Cave
Trap
Beware you don't stuck between its sharp teeth
And its fierce claws
Coma is stupidity!
How foolish your intention will look
When you would like to step on its thresholds
And try to enter its vestibule
And its dark terrifying corridors.

In a coma

Between alertness and absence
Probably you will speak as a great philosopher,
Not like any other philosopher,
Neither before nor after,
Wisdom after wisdom will come out,
From your heavy tongue,
And your hoarse throat,
And your wounded pronunciation,
And your sore lips.

In a coma
You are dead
Yes, you are dead
No one can wake you up
And give your body and soul their life back
Except your lover's tender hand
And her deep heart's music
So listen
So listen
Listen then with all your senses
And with all the remaining breath in your chest,
Then slowly, slowly you will open your eyes
And inevitably you will wake up from your stupid coma.

16-17/5/2020
University Hospital at Bonn, Germany

Translated by Muna Zinati

N. Meera Raghavendra Rao holds an M.A. in English literature and is a freelance journalist, photographer and prolific writer, having authored 10 books both fiction and nonfiction. Her 11th book, *Pinging Pangs* is a collection of 50 verses published in August 2020. She travelled widely within and outside the country.

Granny's Spectacles
Meera Rao

Little Jill a bundle of mischief
Hid her granny's spectacles
Made her run all over
Searching for missing spectacles.
Laughing all the way
Running behind the old lady
At last stood in front of her
Wearing her spectacles.
Frightened everything appeared blurred
Thought her granny disappeared!

Poets of the World

Marcelo Sánchez is from Argentine. He has also lived in the USA and Germany, where he currently resides. He writes poems and short stories.

Notre Dame
Marcelo Sánchez

Something doable
I thought about doing
was standing, during a storm,
to one side of Notre Dame,
and watching the gargoyles
as they regurgitate water nonstop.
I could have done it, but I didn't,
be it because I was on the other side
of Paris (and didn't know how long
the rain would last), or I was nearby
(in the Louvre) but busy
with other things, always aware of
what I was missing, saying to myself:
"Some other time".

Now I shall have to wait
until the Basilica is redone.
When it reopens, I will come back
and see the Madonna in the altar,
but maybe not that pair of paintings
which deserved to be in a museum,
and now –I understand– conserves the Louvre.
Neither do I believe that I shall see again
the wooden sculptures
that surrounded the outside of the choir,
and thus I miss the chance to know
if I would ever like them.

Isn't it an authentic miracle
that the vitraux were saved?
We feared for their safety,
and as soon as we knew they were safe
I thought how great it would be

to see them from short distance.
This is just a dream, because
when Notre Dame reopens,
the vitraux will remain up there,
same as in all these centuries,
indifferent to all of us,
within reach of God.

Photo Credit: Katja Dietermann

From Hamburg, Germany, Gino Leineweber has authored short stories, travel books, biographies, and poetry collections in English and German. He has been awarded several international prizes for his poetry. He has also served as an editor in three international poetry anthologies.

Colette
Gino Leineweber

Colette lives in Paris
Struggles for what has been stolen
From her first husband
The name on the books she wrote
She kisses Missy
Gives the world a stage for truth
Has to live as a vagabond

Colette loves Missy
Lives with beggars and drunkards
Is friend with journalists and writers
The lover from De Jouvenel –
First the father then later the son
She overtrumps the society
With the questioning eye of a wise woman

Colette writes novels
Becomes famous with
Chérie and Awakening Hearts
Composing in it love troubles in purple
And narratives in taboo
In defiance of her time
A woman that is who she thinks she is

A retired banker, C. S. P. Shrivastava studied Sanskrit, English and Psychology at Patna University. He is a sportsman with an understanding of world literature and human values. He views his poems as a process of being natural, a continuous effort to understand the intricacies of the human psyche and nature.

Am I Right?
C. S. P. Shrivastava

I shall not write
About lovelorn lot
The beauteous Sea
The arcane Sky, Moon-
Or, the Nature in
It's grandeur
The verdant Earth-
They dwell in
Marvels though
Aplenty in the Bosoms
Of
Soul's Sublime Glow
It's not the euphony Or
The euphoria
It's not the wars
Fought long ago-
Or the Humanities
Wailings across
The time - slot -
It's the waning
Of virtues-
Out of the mix
The Humanities
Sole Sublime
possessions
Now put to disuse
Or a misuse . . .
To muse miseries
I call upon thee
And hope not
It's dooming plight
Am I right?

Born in Neiba, Dominican Republic, Ramón de Jesús Núñez Duval is writer, historian and poet. He holds a Master's degree in Business Administration and is Specialist in Integrated Management Systems. He has authored *Naked Skin* and *Brief Historical Review of the Bahoruco Province*, and contributed to 30 national and international anthologies.

Let Us Be Reborn
Ramón de Jesús Núñez Duval

We are the breath of peace,
tattooed on the wings of the nightingale,
fiddling in the melody of the air,
which with aroma awakens humanity.

Let us make life, source of light,
draw in pentagram of colors,
the sublime soul of essence and virtue,
where greatness is of hearts.

Molecules of rain, spreading love,
in beautiful wheat fields that kiss the sun,
I do not understand, because it is not possible,
that we all fight for a better world.

The dawn shelters us, because there is God,
the pigeons fly foreshadowing faith,
that one day the planet is protected,
and the human race is reborn.

Nosakhare Collins is a Nigerian poet. He is the author of a poetry chapbook, *a pilgrim of songs* (published in 2018 by SEVHAGE in Nigeria). His poems have appeared in several national dailies and international journals and anthologies.

Nosakhare Tweets, @nosa_collins, and Facebook, Nosakhare Collins

the world's silent when we died
Nosakhare Collins

the sea is bloody & muffled

how many times have you seen an image
of boys at fifty, becoming joyful to stare at;
stinky patch with bullets and scars:
when we stared at it on our secret box.

imagine how the world would look like
if a boy is paralyzed like a broken needle,
and dumped in the gutter to rot;
or find him dead by a mysterious hurricane.

you need not imagine the image you see
of a boy congealed by buzzing bombs;
sprawled on the scarlet bed of a free life,
and holding hands with the sound of silence.

their skins can turn senescent thoughts
fading away like a floating sea;
shows you how to nail sadness into a wanderer's bag,
just to forget the image and remember a boy wanted to turn war for peace.

but remember the naked children laughing
as if there were men,
who shall turn this pearly image of dead bodies,
and grow to remove the rotten leaves of dust.

Dr. Surekha Anandraya Bhat, the daughter of Smt. Vijayalakshmi A. Bhat and Late Shri M.A.V. Bhat, is Associate Dean of Academic affairs at the American University School of Medicine in Aruba. She received the "Best Poet of 2007" prize and the International Poesis award at the Rabindranath Tagore Poetry Contest 2014 from poiesisonline.com.

The Making of the Wise
Surekha Anandraya Bhat

In doom, You pressed on the wound of my heart, like You would, a call bell.
Withdraw in fear or let You in? I opened the door of my heart.
You entered – dusted, swept my heart, washed my soul in its depths;
doom you blew into my soul to produce music joyous!
You gifted me with solitude for I had shy tears,
taught me how to swim in my heart lest despair form an ocean.

A cleaner soul, I've reached a shore, there's still a lot to swim?
My brightened heart, my glowing mind look back to view my past -
on my toiling hands, for a path of joy, You transported bricks of sorrow,
for sorrow is Your classroom for the making of the wise!

Dr. Ranjana Sharan Sinha, professor of English, poet, author and critic, is a prominent voice in English language-Indian Poetry. She has received many poetry awards, and has authored 8 books in different genres and 50 research papers. Her poems have been included in the university syllabus prescribed for the English M.A. program.

A Herculean Odyssey
Dr. Ranjana Sharan Sinha

Seeds of hope
Once planted in the soft hearts
Of machine-like limbs--
Hard and copper-coloured,
Sprouted forth from
A million of obsidian eyes
Opening and closing amid
The flames of gulmohar
And the sunshine of cassia
Adorning the broad, black road
Of the bustling city--
The dream destination of
These migrant workers,
Who came to support families,
Determined to work in sun,
Resolved not to rest in rain!

Today they bear
The brunt of lockdown:
Hungry, homeless, jobless
Onto urban streets--
Once their utopia!
Enforced they embark on
A journey on feet
Back home to their villages
Hundreds of miles away!
Oh, the arduous trek!

Hoisting their children
On their shoulders
They wipe their tears--
They are not afraid
Of the deadly disease:

To them the jaws of hunger
Are mightier than the virus.
Sad and full of uncertainties,
They continue their
Herculean odyssey!

Ro Hamedullah (RH), 33, is a Rohingya poet from Myanmar Country and a teacher by profession. Writing poetry is his passion, but he has also written short stories and quotes. His poems have appeared in numerous anthologies.

Who's the Girl Different from Everyone
Ro Hamedullah

There's a dense cloud of tresses someplace
There is a colourful dress someplace else
There are having a pinkish lips someplace
There's an intoxicating walk someplace else

There is witchcraft in my eyes someplace
There's a fragrance in the body someplace
There are easily bent eyes someplace
There are white arms someplace else

There are so many attractiveness
Who melt moonlight into your eyes
There are so many conversations
Which melt melody into your ears

This one walks with a swirl while
That one walks with a swagger
This one meets in a bashful way while
That one meets with some hauteur

She's like a rose bud in a rose garden,
Different from all the other flowers
What to say, these eyes have seen
Such a breath-taking guise of hers

What a strange freshness she has!
What a beautiful simplicity she has!
What an odd heart-warming grace she has!
What a beautiful attractiveness she has!

There are millions of beauties on every step
But, I'll present my heart as a gift to that one.

Born May 7th, 1979, Craig Alton Kirkland grew up between the Jamaican districts of Featherbed Lane and Frazer's Content and Spanish Town. Popularly known as 'Amaziyah The Great', his contributions to the world of arts by way of his multi-award-winning short films, music, spoken word, music videos have received notable recognition.

Twitter / IG: @preciselygreat
www.facebook.com/thegreatamaziyah

You Will Be OK
Craig Alton Kirkland

Dedicated to Simone Slizy Stewart, and all the women across the world who are experiencing hard times right now.

You are remarkable, You are strong.
You are one of God's greatest gifts, follow H.I.M. you will never go wrong.
You are smart, You are noble,
Pay keen ears to every word that I told you.
The Skies were overcast, then torrential rain for days...
Throughout your darkest moments, you've experienced pain for days.
Cold and bitter, angry and confused,
Be cautious with your steps before you make the wrong moves.
Are you probably feeling a bit empty right now, somewhat unsatisfied?
Fret not! For Jah already sent an angel, to be your travel guide.
You will be ok, okay! Just know that God is real.
After you've overcome that sophisticated phase, it will be the strongest you will ever feel.
You are beautiful, You are sweet,
Trample all hypocrites under your feet.
Be patient and pray more, "You will be OK"
Forget about them who not believe in you, You've got no time to play.
You are a fighter, a survivor who resist to quit,
You are loved, You are a #Queen who deserves lifetime happiness.

From Hyderabad, India, Elizabeth Kurian 'Mona' is a multilingual poet /writer/translator in English, Hindi, Urdu, Malayalam and Telugu. She has thirteen books to her credit, the latest being *The ART AND SCIENCE OF GHAZAL –A Reader's Guide to Urdu Ghazal Appreciation, Scansion and Prosody.*

monaliza.hyd@gmail.com

Ghazal for Ages
Elizabeth Kurian 'Mona'

We have been quite unhappy since ages
We have not laughed heartily since ages

The pandemic has made us ascetics
There has been no friends party since ages

Lost in the mundane vagaries of life
We missed out nature's beauty since ages

So engrossed in their gadgets are kids now
The children's park looks empty since ages

Sky scrapers are mushrooming all around
Sky is seen only partly since ages

Parents now save for their children's future
They have left all luxury since ages

Few visit the inmates of old age homes
Near and dear are too busy since ages

Life has become mechanical 'Mona'
I haven't touched poetry since ages

*The ghazal form comprises independent couplets with a common meter and rhyme scheme. The rhyming words, followed by the refrain appear in both the lines of the first couplet and in the second lines of the others. The name/pen name of the poet is included in the last couplet.

Finlay Hall lives in the North East of Scotland. He first started writing poetry as a teenager in 1970/1. His work has appeared in *Sounds Music Paper*, the *Voices in the Wind* anthology, *Leopard Arts* magazine, and *Spillwords*. He has organized and implemented an event called, "Joined Up Writing and Like a Blot From The Blue".

You Have the Right
Finlay Hall

You have the right to walk the streets
You have the right to love your family
You have the right to go to work
You have the right to be a jerk
You have the right to lie in your bed
You have the right to the thoughts in your head
You have the right to go to the store
You have the right to swim by the shore
You have the right to live your life
You have the right to be with your wife
You have the right to be who you are
You have the right to sit in your car
You have the right to have a drink
You have the right to think how you think
You have the right to protest and march
You have the right to make your mark
You have the right to go to your church
You have the right to not be smirched
You have the right to turn your back
You have the right to not get attacked
You have the right to stay out of jail
You have the right to try and fail
You have the right to remain silent
But anything you say may be used in evidence against you
You have the right to a lawyer
If you haven't got one, a court appointed lawyer will be given to you
You have the right to not speak
You have the right to be meek
You have the right to be heard
You have the right to be a nerd
You have the right to be wrong
You have the right to be strong

You have the right to take the knee
You have the right to have the same rights as me
You have the right to vote
You have the right to be remote
You have the right to draw back
You have the right to be black
You have the right to survive
You have the right to remain alive

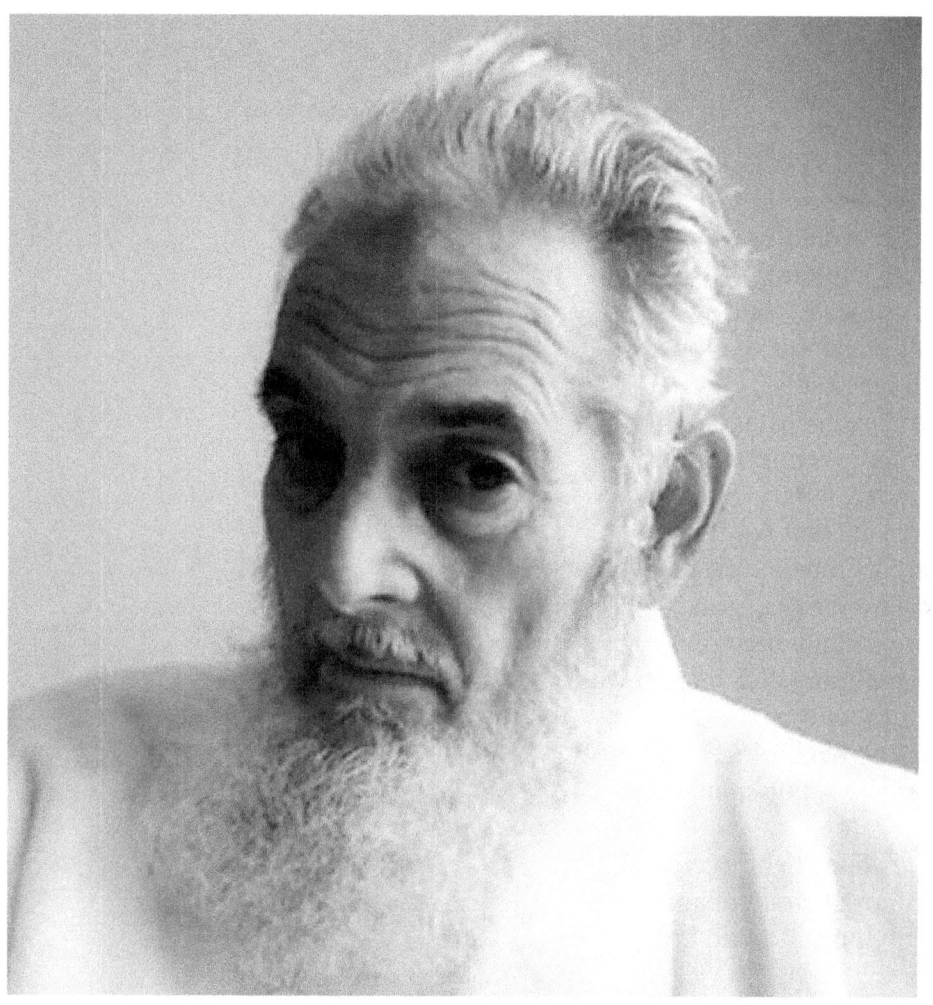

Born and raised in Brooklyn, NYC, Shareef Abdur-Rasheed, AKA "Zakir Flo", is a Vietnam era veteran, human rights activist and a percussion artist. He writes conscious poetry and socio-political commentaries, has authored *Poetic Snacks 4 the Conscious Munchies* and contributed to numerous international anthologies. Shareef is married with 9 children, 44 grandchildren and 4 great grandchildren.

https://www.facebook.com/shareef.abdurrasheed1
https://zakirflo.wordpress.com
http://www..com/shareef-abdur-rasheed.php

please stay close to me
Shareef Abdur-Rasheed

your majesty he who
monopolized legitimacy
over all other would be kings
they have no supremacy,
them who come, go fade away
all fake comparatively
their death inevitably
hangs over head constantly
they were not given immortality
their stay is temporary
they were made that way
by he who fashioned universe,
ocean, sky, mountains, seas,
you and me and all creation
just by proclaiming "BE" and it was,
and it is and it will be
he who has no beginning,
no end was not begotten nor does
he beget
he (Allah) is one (1) he is eternal,
there is nothing that compares
in a class by himself period.

he is not creation he is thee creator
him alone worthy of worship
far removed from taqhut (false deities)
the likes of which is attributed to thee
by folk misguided
those who take truth and hide it
instead take fake
try to disguise it until that day
comes their way and all souls
will realize that truth

prevails over falsehood
cannot be watered down
to appease men's needs
fulfill their greed, bring ease
to the fact they don't believe,
didn't heed

far removed is he from all needs
not like his creation
who have limitations
creator does not need creation
creation needs creator

do not worship any creation
nor their false gods,
imitations all fake!!
lands, nations, tribes,
cultures created by man
including their flags
are not sacred, holy
nor do they deserve
praise, devotion, glory
they are all things of man
only creator deserves,
praise, glory, worship,
devotion, submission

mankind's tribal cultures,
traditions
designed to deter one from
giving all praise, glory, worship,
devotion, submission
to only Allah*(swt) exclusively
the only purpose for which he
created thee
thus hindering mankind

from the straight path
that on which creator bestowed
his eternal grace
not of them who went astray
ultimately receive eternal
damning disgrace

*(swt) = all glory to Allah.

food4thought = education
Zakir Flo

Poetry... The Best of 2020

Ananda Nepali, ICPI's Culture Ambassador for Nepal, East India and Tibet, is Director of Policy Research and Consulting Services Nepal; initiator for Nepal's Dalit Dignity First Campaign that works to eliminate the South Asian caste/racial discrimination; [. . .], and an environmental activist [. . .]. He writes articles, poems, and research papers for youth empowerment and social change.

The Best of 2020
Ananda Nepali

I believe that it's new life when I entered in 2020,
COVID19 taught us that we should learn how to live in new life.
I hope that through people's eyes, you only see me.
I heard that World needs to operate eco-friendly,
That People's voice is similar to that of Mercy,
Am starting to get a good vibe, like New World,
Honestly tell me why people don't understand about world now,
I buy fruits and vegetables but at the market there is local products,
I've been sending message my doctor friends, they are so busy to serve patient devotedly
before shared with me that I should have you daily by my side,
Key words are love, care and humanity for world.
I believe that COVID19 taught people to re-think the way we worked, studied, lived,
There are thousands of stories of solidarity and resourcefulness,
Stories of neighbours supporting each other, of small businesses finding ways,
This single, simple change has sparked a worldwide love of eBooks and webinar.
To serve their customers that turns my world on,
I love that and so much more,
I love the way technology moves humanity forward.
For that and so much more,
Allow me leave this poetic note,
I hope we'll be taking some of the new lessons we've learned with us.
I'm going to continue to support vulnerable/marginalized communities
    and local businesses.
So, take my words creatively,
My hope faithfully and take some notes,
The Invisible determinations, with visible ideals.

Dr. Tarana Turan Rahimli, an Azerbaijani poet, writer, journalist and literary critic, has a doctorate in Philological Sciences. Associate Professor of World Literature Chair of Azerbaijan State Pedagogical University, she has authored 8 books and more than 400 articles. Her work has been published in more than 35 countries.

I Grew up
Tarana Turan Rahimli

I was left on the crossroads,
I grow up choosing my own way.
I passed through the aches
That filled into my inside.

I was interested with a strange wish,
I directed towards light and sound.
I drunk off the love
I grew up drinking such loves.

I took hands of the expectation,
I was lost in the corners of life.
I cut the grief to my height
I grew up in this way.

My spirit was invaded thousand times,
I took shelter only in the hemistiches.
A fire was made inside of my heart
But I didn't burn, I grew up being experienced.

Laure Charazac is a French poet who has authored *Voyages of a Loving Soul* (in English and French, published by Inner Child Press International). Her poems have appeared in several anthologies. To her, poetry represents the most beautiful in our existence.

My Love
Laure Charazac

I look into your deep blue eyes,
Then I am not in reality anymore,
Now all you have to do is close the door,
And let me invite you to love's paradise.
I caress your face with my fingertips,
Temptation is glowing on your silky l
I cannot resist the way they're smiling at me,
Slowly I get closer and kiss them passionately,
This is a beautiful moment for you and me only.
I take you in my arms and feel the warmth of your chest,
Listen to my whispers in your ears and forget about the rest.
Let me take you to the heavens of love,
Passion is waiting for us above.

Ann Christine Tabaka, a Pushcart Prize in Poetry nominee and the winner of Spillwords Press 2020 Publication of the Year, was featured in Sweetycat Press' "Who's Who of Emerging Writers 2020". She is the author of 12 poetry books and won numerous awards for her work which has appeared in international anthologies.

And Still, I Had These Dreams
Ann Christine Tabaka

And still, I had these dreams.
Dreams of grandeur, iced in white frosting.
Waking to the truth.
A truth that no longer resides
beside the waterfall of hope.
Reaching for conclusions,
my eyes do not open fully.
Yawning my farewell
to all the glittery trinkets
set forth before the illusion.
A time so long ago,
that memories fail to adhere.
Buried alive in anticipation,
of a tomorrow that will not be.
Sweet songs of triumph
written in the icing,
now melting from neglect.
The night, no longer young,
as I am not.
We join hands in celebration,
the letting go of false intent.
Closed eyes to deep breath,
I succumb to a reality set before me.
And still, I had these dreams.

David Winship is a native of the southern mountains, in the region of east Tennessee/Southwest Virginia where he has lived most of his life. His career has been in education. He coordinates the Appalachian Center for Poets and Writers, operating from The Arts Depot in Abingdon, Virginia.

Where Heaven and Hills . . .
David Winship

Where heaven and hills collide
the jagged western range
the sawteeth of the southwest
the rounded ranges of the southern mountains
there is where my horizon hangs
in balance.

Where heaven and hills connect
life cycles airborne from terra firma
evaporate from substance
sustenance from substrate
there is where my hope rises
in balance.

Where heaven and hills kiss
a touching peck in clouds concealed
a firm embrace in contrast unconcealed
a fiery power as lightning strikes
there is where my love lies
in balance.

Poetry... The Best of 2020

Ibaa Ismail is a Syrian American poet. Her talent started to shine when she was an undergraduate student. She has authored eleven collections of poetry. She received her latest award from the Ministry Culture of Egypt during the Creative Arabic Women Forum which was held in Cairo in December, 2019.

On the Borders of Ignition
Ibaa Ismail

Clouds, sadness
and a wave of memories,
rain of heavy eagerness
over the language's sweet summit . . .
And the red letters,
sound their pulses and anthem together.
Infatuated with a wistful memory,
I vanish, still with a hope for a future of
illuminated nights.

***

I am a rose in your shade,
dominating like your sun.
When I look for your fruit in my blood,
I run tenderly . . .
Am I seeing your brightness,
flourishing within us like others?
Or am I going to look for my rose
in your open prairies? . . .
Or in my own depth
Or in my own voice?
Our infatuation has been hanged
on a blaze
to enlighten our sky.

***

Tell me,
How my bewildered bee,
Returned to its most captivating garden?
Tell me,
how could you return to me,
like a cloud,
that entered the stars,

as if they were digging at a mine
defiance in the dust of each strike
And a gush of your beaming glow.

***

Like the fire,
which was floating over the surface of water,
The universe had become
and the universe had receded
and my blood had been shining like a daylight

***

Thorns are bleeding out my heart
and shouting to me:
SCATTER.
and
BREAK DOWN.
But the roses . . .
where are the roses?
Roses are for madness!

I shout to the thorns:
I have a surrendered nation,
and my wounds have ignited poems.
Their fires stay still
to make my blood a branched nation.

***

Bleeding has stopped,
and the Earth is the storm of existence . . .
The rain has stopped
and the Earth is the mother of blood.
Our pain was flowing
like a vision gathering us
as a wing of a sun
Or a prairie,
rising to reach the golden horizon

***

*(Ishtar) presented to me,
some of the horses' defiance
and I sprinted in a glowing fantasy.
A gazelle in my blood is racing me,
then embracing me,
and sharing with me
your shine.
Oh Gazelle . . .

***

Ishtar presented to me her features,
a sky on the way to ignition.
Here we were united,
pruning our spirit's sprouts.
You planted me,
a flame of a tender pain
and a flower of a tormented yet dignified silence.
You planted me:
a lightened inscription,
and scattered your spirit.
In my blood: ambition
and a radiating spirit!

*Ishtar is a primary Mesopotamian goddess associated with love and war.

From Bangladesh, poet Shakil Kalam is Central Banker, Corporate Governance Specialist, researcher, and child-litterateur. He has been writing stories, poems, essays and columns. His published books number thirty. He has participated in seminars, symposia and conferences in various countries across the globe. He is Honorary Fellow of a Foundation.

Speaking of Artists and Art
Shakil Kalam

Artist, you draw pictures, mixing the sweetness of the mind
You are an artisan, you know the magic of art.
Draw pictures of nature - love the heavens,
Draw a picture of war, the fall of human civilization.
Draw a picture of famine; Pictures of life struggle,
A timeless picture of Zainul's fifties.
Disasters, pictures of epidemics; Lamentations of humanity,
Introduce the moon and the sun to the glory of art.
Draw pictures of human class inequality,
Give analogies to create awareness among people.
Paint a beautiful lady, a worshiper of beauty,
Leonardo da Vinci's Mona-Lisa is still world famous.
Oil paintings, watercolors, sketches, how much more,
Pictures of life, abstract pictures, primitive, surreal pictures,
Modern, post-modern pictures and timeless pictures.
Oh, artist, have you been able to draw a picture of the soul?

Ibrahim Honjo, a Canadian poet /writer, has authored 30 books in English and Serbo-Croatian and contributed to 40 anthologies. His work has appeared in numerous publications. Some of his poems have been published in their Italian, Korean, Spanish, Mongolian, Slovenian, Polish, German and Bahasa (Malesia) translations. He has received several poetry awards.

Arrival Out of Ignorance
Ibrahim Honjo

For whom the church bells toll
for whom is a muezzin praying from the minaret
on Friday at twelve
for whom I cried that Friday

who are they calling at this time swollen from pain
which I hugged with the first sob

I arrived at the right time, they said
when spring began to mature
they gave me the name of my grandfather
who was swallowed by the great war

all wars are great and blood-stained

I was born after the last great war
I cry for all the wars of the past and future

do the bells toll to announce my birth
or some new great war that will eat me

does the muezzin pray on the minaret
to announce a new upcoming bloodshed
or just advertise my crying

I'm here and I do not know why
my mother did not promise me anything
she only held me on her bosom
tears came out of her eyes
because
she had nothing in her breasts to feed me with

my father was somewhere, carving stone
and he looked on this day through one eye

they promise everyone that it will be better

and it is always better for someone
after great wars

God has never stopped the bloodshed
by brainwashing
they awake the imagination of the population
and with fear, they complete their promises
everything is imagination except my birth

I really did not want to come here
and witness the self-destruction of mankind
somebody planted a cuckoo's egg on me
which I sensed at birth

only my mother and father
rejoiced in my first cry
afterward, everything was according
to the unwritten rules of the universe

it's time to go to that gray stone
and dream in peace
about the peace destroyed
in the name of the Creator of the Worlds
and non-existent democracy

the myth of peace and peacemakers
remains only a myth
because
peace can only be made by producers of war

bells will continue to toll
and a muezzin will pray
sheep will continue to follow a bell-ringer ram

I watch the ship sink without the captain
and the helmsman

I'm singing "The Internationale"

Dr. Annie Pothen, Professor at Osmania University Hyderabad, India, has a brilliant academic track. She was awarded a Certificate of Excellence for Paradoxist Poetry from the University of Arizona, USA and was a member of the American Bibliographical Institute. She has authored two volumes of poetry that are available online.

A Minor Blessing
Annie Pothen

'Know Thyself' preached
the philosopher sage.
So, study your image visage,
in a bright, clear mirror.
Critically assess the reflection
gazing back at you.
you will at once discover
how the highlights
of your countenance
prompts you to feel
somewhat like Narcissus,
the handsome Greek lad
who took immense pride
in his appearance.
Unlike him, however,
one would do well
to analyze one's
characteristic traits,
revel in strengths
though wisdom lies
in tracking drawbacks
converting them
into strengths,
so we become better
with each passing day.
Be a minor blessing
to the universe.
Cultivate an altruistic
human spirit.
Embrace humanity
in UNITY, PEACE And LOVE!!

Dr. Aneek Chatterjee is a poet and academic from India. His work has been appeared in reputed literary magazines and poetry anthologies across the globe. He has authored 13 literary and academic books. He was a Fulbright Visiting Professor at the University of Virginia, USA. His poetry has been archived at Yale University.

Pains
Aneek Chatterjee

Pains have many exits,
but only a single depository,
hidden inside bones.
In that invisible pot, the old lady
unloads lonely winter evenings
in candle light
Here the barren fields whisper
melancholy after every harvest
& wrinkles around doused eyes
practice laughter surreptitiously.

Pains have many languages,
but only one page
where we scribble colored
graphs of monitors from
white, cold beds.

Pains have many becks,
but only one small pond,
where drops are stored
in winter & fall, spring
& summer

Vandana Kumar is a teacher of French, translator and recruitment consultant in New Delhi. She is also a poet with her work having been appeared in numerous national and international journals. Poetry for her is her stress buster, her flight of fancy and strangely, what keeps her rooted too.

An Outsider
Vandana Kumar

Hadn't society
Distanced itself already?
From the cries for help
From the neighbor at 3am

Hadn't we washed of?
All responsibility
For harvests
Of rot

We kept the mandatory 6ft
From reports
Of daily crimes
Of hate
Of stratum
And skin
That looked different
Of enemy state
Infested with familiar sameness
And yet . . .

Along came a virus
Making it official
Man for only
One man
Fed on 'Me love'
'Social distancing'
Just a hashtag

We were already
Flawed souls
In self-owned apartments
Rented bodies

A society
Looking at universe
With an outsider's gaze

Poetry... The Best of 2020

Born in a village of Bangladesh, the bilingual poet Rehanul Hoque is a worshipper of beauty and wants to promote beauty and truth together through the appreciation of beauty, by means of poetry. He dreams of a future ruled only by love.

Nothing Makes Happy
Rehanul Hoque

Now a day nothing makes me happy
Bunch of roses, sweet sunshine, water drops
Grey desert, cold breeze and green land
Beauty pageant, glistening stars----- nothing

Walking across the valley I met a peddler
He said: Look over there
Earlier hills were not like these
They looked like brides wearing vermilion
Music could be heard from that desolate heath
At midnight there were meteor showers
Breaking silence a bird used to shriek
Now nothing makes the peddler happy

A bee buzzing around complained:
The star has fallen from its orbit
Long since there is no rain
Flowers bloom in the arid desert
Followers are decorating a coffin with flower
Now nothing makes the bee happy

A bird was flying nearby
The bird told:
In the coming winter many princes will visit this place
Some Houbara bustard live in those tall trees
The locality will be developed
There will be avenues, stadiums and large shopping malls
Now nothing makes the bird happy

Few steps ahead
A small stone on wayside looked sad
'Stone, what caused you such pain?'
The stone replied mournfully-

We are three siblings
Now the older one resides in the White house
People say she is happy
The stair that His Excellency steps down every morning
She enhances its glamour
The middle one is in Aleppo
Now she is too old to be recognized
And the youngest stone herself is too lonely
Now nothing makes the small stone happy

A gust of wind blew over
The wind whispered:
Do you know once wind and water were true lovers-
'Single entity, single soul'
Many nations, many civilizations through rise and fall
Bear witness to their historic love,
Today the age-old civilization declares
The share of water is the hottest topic for politics
Wind and water became separated
Now nothing makes the wind happy.

Rosy Lidia Alosious, a professor, passionate thinker and writer, is an expert in Communicative English, Soft Skills Development, Public Speaking Skills training, for which she has conducted workshops. Many of her creative writings have appeared in renowned national and international publications. She is the recipient of the 2019-20 Best Researcher Award.

rosylidia.si@gmail.com

Hiatus
Rosy Lidia Alosious

The wheels of dawn and dusk
keep churning
through the paths of life.

To hold on to a break
seemed quite impossible.

Part of routine,
have things coursed in:
to be the routine.

Work ceased not
family time, however prearranged
ended up a mess
due to lining up work schedules.

Now, a forced time,
to spend with family.
Quantity, again a constraint
as work from home presses.

Yet, some quality time assured
if planning slides in,
appropriately as it should be.

Hiatus,
the break to rejuvenate,
to recreate the lost moments
and to feel afresh
to face the future.

Tapas Dey, a teacher, has been living in India, West Bengal, Mathabhanga since his childhood. He takes interest in writing poems in English under the inspiration of his father. His first poetry book is titled *A Green Canvas*.

An Unspoken Pain
Tapas Dey

Soldiers arrayed in unbound jungle apparels,
armed to teeth,
are confirmed standing army for their country.

A clear signal on the wire, armistice.

On the border, under a thatching beside a tree
a certain time offered them earnest repose.

A little far, from across the border,
seen was a little girl coming on gingerly steps
with armful of red and white roses.

One soldier's sharp sight fell upon her,
soon stood and a few steps ahead to her.
Given one rose of peace to each one soldier
each one gave her fond hug.

But the last one soldier noticed
blood oozing from a cut on her pink palm.
Then was her asked how happened.
Pointed out by her is a pricking-wire-net behind.

Alicja Maria Kuberska, awarded Polish poet, novelist, journalist, and editor, is ICPI's Cultural Ambassador for Poland and Eastern Europe, member of the Polish Writers Associations, IWA Bogdani (Albania), Soflay Literature Foundation's Directors' Board, and Our Poetry Archive (India). Her poems have been translated into many languages and appeared in numerous anthologies and magazines.

A Philosopher and a Poet
Alicja Maria Kuberska

They met between heaven and earth
at the place where time and matter are irrelevant,
at a higher level of abstraction.
They overcame the barriers of the real world.

He brought a white canvas and philosophical maxims.
She brought the paint brushes
and a handful of dreams in words.
They painted the picture in many shades of blue.
They poured their thoughts and feelings into the ether.

He sketched the outlines of life with a bold navy blue line.
She filled the background with gentle azure brushes.
Together they added a few colorful spots of astonishment.
His eyes are hazel and hers are green

Gobinda Biswas, an Indian poet, has composed more than 435 poems between 2013 and October, 2020. He has four books to his credit, *The Sunny Poems* (86 poems), *The Universal Poems* (90 poems), *The Eternal Poems* (110 poems) and *The Global Poems* (114 poems).

The Sapling Prays
Gobinda Biswas

I'm a very little sapling so uncared
But I can make you really happy,
If you protect me with a strong fence
And take care of me like your baby.

Please kill me not, politely I pray
For I want to live among you,
I'm your true friend since long
But you've forgotten me, so I rue.

If you love me a bit, O friend
I'll return it in hundred times,
At first I'll give you fresh oxygen
Without it no animate survives.

Like the ladylove to her Wight
I implore, please love me a bit,
I will give you flowers and fruits
Along with mother's shadow, I admit.

I will protect soil with my roots
I'll provide food, clothing and shelter,
When I will die like hermit Dadhichi
I will give you fuel and furniture.

Ajanta Paul, a widely-published poet, short story writer and critic from Kolkata, India, has been in academia for ages and has returned to her first love – writing. She earned her Ph.D. in English from Jadavpur University in the 1990s and is currently working at the Women's Christian College in Kolkata.

The Lifting of the Curse
Ajanta Paul

When did the curse lift
Like fog off a hazy vale,
Revealing layers of settlement
Lying clustered
In the soul?

Was it a word
That did the trick?
A smile, perhaps, that played
Around the lips of things cosmic?
Which was the key that fitted the lock?

A gust of wind
Knocked open the door of fate
Freeing the prince
From an eternity of entrapment
In amphibian enchantment.

Nandita De nee Chatterjee is a writer and freelance journalist for *Ex-Economic Times*. She has contributed to 22 anthologies, including *30 Best Poets*, *Sea*, *Christmas in My Heart*, *Moonlight*, *ALS's Asia & Bilingual Anthology*, *Writers' Haven*, *Rewrite the Stars*, *Love Thy Mother*, *The Real Hero*, *Lockdown Diaries*, *Born to Dream* [. . .].

About Us
Nandita De nee Chatterjee

He strode down the silent
empty road
his stride firm
steely-grey eyes stern
looking straight on
strong, striking
handsome
past the little girl
and her smaller friend
not a glance or nod
toward their eager
faces
and childish hellos.

But the little girl looked on
proud
and on later
as the girls around her grew
as he with his aquiline looks
and inscrutable aura
went on his way
impervious to childish admiration
or the little girls' adulation.

He seldom spoke
his voice never rose by a decibel
his anger never worded
but
his stern calm
volatile by its sheer intensity
shattered into thousands of
little bits
her every budding waywardness
and she knew she had to try
harder
and much harder

to be even a bit of him.

Oh! if only his unsurmountable
strength
the unfailing step in life
unaffected
by the murky wastage
of greed, power, wealth,
sickness, sin, strewn around
the steely glance
always way ahead
unseeing, unknowing
that it's a tough world
he's been walking
these seventy years up.

Unaccepting
that there can be travails of life
to falter the strong step.

If only a little
of this sheer force
of strength
infused the air
through which he walked.

The little girl couldn't
remain little for long
the childish joys
of cuddling up in his
armchair
had to go
but she knew
she was the only one
who could have done so.

Who could sit on his lap
on a moon-drenched
Laxmi Purnima night,

the holy full moon capturing their
smiles
in the dark balcony,
keeping him company
as he shied away
from the festive friends
and feasts at his place.

Who could walk through
those silent dark roads
in no-man's land
learning lessons of life
handed down,
few words
of kindness, correctness
and valour
which would see her through life.

He says little even now
sometimes
only to the boys in the house
while
she craves to know
every detail
every little bit of
his pride and glory
his Air Force days
his unfaltering
dedication to service
his vision
which served him right
and those around him.

His steely glance is
sometimes a little forgetful
now
the fast clasp on the
little hand once
somewhat weaker

one arm shakes incessantly
and his lines are a little deeper.

She knows he is not
feeling so strong
she cries for he
never says now
those words of wisdom
to steer her from
the darkness around.

For she's a grown-up now,
but his strong persona
which cast life's most lasting
influence on her
still remains
and though it's tough
very tough
to see him weaker
in years.

He still gives
support
strength
and silent love
to all those he holds.

And she still derives
a lot that she forgot
to take
those childish years.

For Dad, there's much
more
that she needs
still from you.

Vidya Shankar, poet, writer, yoga practitioner, mandala artist, a Human Library "book", and English teacher, is the author of two poetry books, *The Flautist of Brindaranyam* and *The Rise of Yogamaya*. A recipient of literary awards, Vidya is one of the editors of *Kavya-Adisakrit*, an imprint of Adisakrit Publishing House.

The Moonlight Sonata
Vidya Shankar

Astride their motorbike, the lovebirds jaunted
Along the promenade by the beach
Her hero holding the handlebars of his vehicle
And she him, her arms around his slender waist
They rode through the perturbed traffic
Blissfully unaffected by the rush.
His eyes were on the road ahead
And his mind very conscious of safe driving
But his heart was upon his sleeve, his left one
For it was upon his left shoulder
She had placed her chin, and notwithstanding the solid helmet
She was whispering love cajoles into his waiting ears.

Moon, he spotted them from up afar
Through the branches of the trees that lined the pavement
His heart skipping a beat, he raced up, and ahead too
So he may see her better, and be seen . . . by her
Alas! she didn't . . . so enveloped was she
With the man she shared conjugal moments
Not just on the motorbike but all her life with.

He, the celestial orb, was up there for all to see
Glowing against a cerulean satin
Of a balmy night of lunar fullness
A luminous alluring seductive giant pearl
That poets languished their versified thoughts upon.
Oh! But to her, he came not at all within her ken
Her entire attention orbiting her married love only
As they wheeled through the traffic, a romantic earthen ride.

Yet once she did turn her eyes toward him
Ever so briefly, but ever so disinterestedly
A faint glance that meant, well, nothing at all—
Dark desolation clouded his radiant full visage

Darkened, he hid his bright self behind curtains grey
Peeping yet not so, hoping against hope
That she would reciprocate his lucent love for her.

Till he saw them turn into the road that led
To the abode they called their heaven
Out came he, beaming, from behind the clouds
Presented himself in full view of her sight
Putting on his best bright face with all his might—
Not in vain were his efforts, for, as she got off the motorbike
She looked ahead . . . and saw him, placed as he was
At vantage.

It was just a minute, yet seemingly an eternity
When eyes met eyes . . .
A moment in which all the sounds of the moving world
Around her came to a mute.
Her iris held only the iridescence
Of the heavenly light shining brighter now
And her breath, a zephyr, calm and composed
She knew there was a blessing to come
So, with eyes locked still, she drew her husband to her
Hand in hand they stood, in gratitude, receiving
The luminous divine Love that embosomed them
Hand in hand they stood, in prayerful solace
Aroused by the Grace bestowed upon them
Hand in hand they stood, not twain anymore, but as one
Neither man nor woman, but as light
An illumination meant to brighten
Many a darkened souls to smile
Hand in hand they stood, a conspiracy of eternity
So the world may know that what makes it go around
Are not its laws of motion and fixed notion
Hand in hand they stood, a reflection, a celebration
An eternal ethereal story of Love!

Poets of the World

Robert Gibbons, a native Floridian, came to New York City in 2007. His first book, *ClosetotheTree*, was published by the New York-based Three Rooms Press in 2012. His recent work has been released by Expound, Promethean, Turtle Island Quarterly, KillerWhale, Inner Child Press International and Suisun Valley Review.

Oh, the Ocean
Robert Gibbons

I heard the story. The man named John wanted to proselytize on a restricted island
located off the coast of the Indian Ocean. And the people were called the Sentinelese
a 55,000 years old civilization that refuse to conform.
They were not willing to modernize.
Not willing to gentrify into a world that is as fast and as long as it will last.

The people, the Sentinelese, considered tribal or primitive
or any of those textbook phrases
are not inhibited, are not limited to our idea of society and what is wrong with keeping
your person close, they will not be coerced, to innovate, not the will of the people
to invite a resort, a casino, a development, a cohort of island with miniature golf cars

to live beneath the radar, without car or airplane, without chaos or the insane,
not the paved roads of our conquerors, not the blasphemous loads of steel
or machinery, the Sentinelese, their animistic bodies are marvels for the curious,
for the purity of Christendom, an art object
for the museum cabinet, maybe a display for the zoo a crew of elephants domesticated

appropriate without social, or economic, or political, non- status seekers, cultural phonics
and his name was John, he rented a boat to traverse the mighty waters, the restricted area
of our histories, the Nicobar, the Andaman, the Indian, all the names we call,
and tried to pay them, tried to pray for them, tried to anoint them into the New World,
in the Old world

would travel by canoe with Bible in hand, a man of land of country,
of privilege, of means
in between this heaven we call hell, this Dante's purgatory, his Christian-missionary self
came to tell them about Jesus, about the crucifix, as if Columbus is not in our thought
bought and sold small pox, as if the Santa Maria, Nina, and the Pinta, did not arrive
the Amerigo Vespucci in him, with all the self- regard for his nation, John-the-Conqueror
John-on-the-Cross met them, the Sentinelese, a people, a warrior, a sect, a tribe,
an animist,
a blame, for the loot, for the booty, for the conspiracy, for the piracy,
to tell them about God
far from their island, a God that is a star, in this myriad planet,
in this pantheon

Poets of the World

of poly-god, and polytheism, a mob of them with bow and arrow, call him Roque, or her
Crow- mother, call them devastation or destruction, John-the Conqueror, his Bible
Shot him back to the ocean, back to the baptism of Pochantas,
shot him back to the Crucified, like Calvary, a blood bath as communion,
a blood bath as indigenous, a dragging

a hanging, an insurrection beyond border, beyond state of the union,
a mutiny like Amistad
his body a breach, a reach beyond latitude, beyond ship wreck,
the tectonic plates will implode
and the land will return Pangea. Will Gawanda, will glaciate,
will ice over in the kingdom come
will rain murder, and trial and tribulation,
will be 40 days of Noah on the rainy tide,

when the ocean becomes land and the land become ocean, Oh, ocean, drown me
Oh ocean, flood your gates, make me mud lotus, great fertilizer, great murderer
My body will be like his a decomposition, great murderer, unction me to the great
Beyond, transpose me into plankton, into amoeba, into keel, and then John saw

And number that no man could number, his body the great revelator, Oh, the
Ocean is mother ocean her porous landscape, the ways she mates life and death
The way breath suffocates, and the consulate wants his body back, but he is taken
he is flight and elegy, when our body is baptized in Jesus's name, Oh, ocean, submerged
in your liquid grave, the waves are contentious, the moon and tide roar back
to God, Oh, ocean is the photosynthesis to mention when my body becomes
ecosystem or am I a philistine as caverns of the body becomes sunshine, part
pine needle, stymied energy, pent up in me, oh, ocean, the part of me to be

pure, water, pure whisper, and sound, Rumi's water wheel, my trajectory
protected landscape. I can be so shallow as I follow hegemony. Ocean, feel
the motion as I caracole your water, may I farrago, may I embargo in you. Oh,
sacred space, O, Ocean, O, Soul, mold me of the amphibious and indigenous

humbled by you. O, Ocean, O, Soul, still in search of the old gold, will take back
my nativism in your caverns of blue and infinite where we live only as tenement
on earth, O, Ocean, only death, only death.

Tangirala Sree Latha, Associate Professor, a bilingual poet, short story writer and translator, writes in English and Telugu. Her poems have appeared in national and international publications. She regularly contributes to ICPI's anthologies, Muse India, The Criterion, Cape Comorin Publisher, GIPF-Guntur, and *Amaravati Poetic Prism*. She has authored *VOICED THOUGHTS* and 57 research papers.

The Journey of the Virus from A To Z
Dr. Tangirala Sree Latha

An avalanche of apprehension and angst
Bombarded the beautiful blue-ball's breath
Causing calamity, commotion and chaos
Devastating delight, dream and delectation
Engulfing energy, ecstasy and exuberance
Flooding with fear, fever and frightful frailty
Governing the globe grumpily with grudge
Haunting the hopeless with heinous and horrific hope
Importing immigrants and intense impediments
Jeopardizing their jittery jinxed lives
Knocked down by knifelike knees and killing knuckles
Lamenting at the lamely limping listless life
Many mighty minds' mellowing motherliness
Nurtured the numerous needy and the neglected
Optimism originating from outstanding orbits
Patience to persevere the piercing pain
Quality life quenching the quantity in queue
Readily recalled rulers' reasonable rationale
Sensible subjects supported to sustain and soar
Truly taught therapeutic tactics to thousands
Ultimately united the Universe to unfold
Valiant vibes to vanquish the villainous virus
With warring will and wondrous weapons to win
Xenophobia expelled by xenial expressions
Yearning for yesteryears' yonder youthful yell
Zestful and zealous to zip-up the zinged zones

Padmini Janardhanan is rehabilitation psychologist, educational consultant, corporate consultant for Learning and Development, and counsellor for career, personal and family disquiets. She strongly believes that literature shapes and influences personality; so, she uses poetry, songs, quotes, and stories for counselling and training. She writes poetry and prose.

padjan1976@gmail.com

Born Free
Padmini Janardhanan

Born free, yet we live in chains.
Powerless? Feeble? helpless?
Indolence? or just habit?

Born free occurs – it's a gift from nature
Living free emerges – with effort
Conscious, steadfast, deliberate

Fear of oppression, victimization
Fueled by helpless incompetence
Dissolves with supportive confidence.

Freedom – political, gender, social
And for all other faces of freedom
First among them - personal freedom.

Born free, yet layered with bondage
One doesn't achieve or obtain freedom
Only chisels away the layers flung

The chisel too is born with us
Potentially powerful
Awaits its release from disuse

Let the divine grant us fortitude
The ability and the strength too
To work with the chisel diligently

Elvirawati Pasila completed her education in the Department of French literature at Hasanuddin University in Makassar, South Sulawesi in Indonesia. Currently, she resides in Tana Toraja and works as a teacher at Junior High Schools. Her poems have appeared in numerous anthologies.

elvirpasila@gmail.com

Light After the Storm
Elvirawati Pasila

I walk under the sun
Greet the sky decorated with clouds
Frolic with the wind that blew my hair

I walked following my shadow
And your face is blocking my steps
Why always be there when my feet step
While your time is over
Please go . . .
So that the soles of my feet do not stumbled
Don't block me with a mirage
Love is no longer there for you
My life has gone on without you

The storm was over
The storm that you brought to ravage my ark
And in confusion the rays come
Show the direction where to go
Even though I limped off
But I was able to hold on and go on again.

Poetry... The Best of 2020

MTK resides in the South Bronx. She has been featured, hosted and produced events from 2010 to the present. Her first poetry book, *Eyez of the Sister*, was published in 2010. Monthly, she is the host at Landmark Nama Harlem; now virtually on zoom due to the COVID-19 pandemic.

Virgo's Breeze
Marilyn Thomas-King

Touches my soul
Warm yet cool
Comfortable
That's what we (2×) do . . .

Summer's ending
Covid-19 not slowing down
Yet we are here . . .
Continuing to fight
Survival instincts are in charge . . .

This Virgo breezes is cooling
All of us down
Mr. Fall letting us feel
He is back in town – town – town . . .

And my spirit & soul
Dances and feeds
Nuturiments for your body and mind . . .

Close your eyes
And let Virgo's breeze
Calm you peacefully down . . .

Rofiat Omobolanle Kareem is a Nigerian writer, poet, and lover of language. She lives in the southwestern Nigeria, where she writes from. She currently studies English language at Obafemi Awolowo University, Ile-Ife.

Homeward
Rofiat Omobolanle Kareem

When a girl asks what home is
I tell her home is many wagging tongues moulding clay . . .

Home is a cracked foot
that beds us on uneven lines
Mama's voice is a collage of haunting memories,
shards of broken dreams that lodge in my body.
I pack my bags to head home
and My ears sing songs of fire
that melt my tongue into tears.
I look at my skin
and try to peel the print of his name;
But isn't home a place you wear an elephant's skin over dry bones?
they once told me that home is the place a traveler packs from
that home is also the place he lands
they just didn't say that the flight is never mapped.
So as i journey again to my father's lounge,
i try to picture what home is like;
i see that home is a blind woman
and i, a broken road
that home is a mute man
i, a dejected abode of words
Nobody leaves home
unless home is a dwelling of snakes
No, unless snakes do bite
unless bites are deadly.

So when a girl asks me what home is
I will tell her that home is a girl's place till death.

Poetry... The Best of 2020

Divya Sinha hails from Delhi, India. After 30 years of service with the central government, she has retired in May, 2015. She has had many stories and poems running in her head for years which she has begun to put to paper now. These include poems for the disadvantaged children she teaches.

Waiting for the Fireflies
Divya Sinha

Rain has ceased;
The evening is coming on,
Swarms of dragonflies in a merry- go –round,
It is growing dark but the sky looks blue.

Luminescent, glowing moon,
Wisp of cloud floating across;
The comforting Venus,
A few stars like French knots in the sky;
It just needs a firefly or two to make it magical.

The season of rains has gone by.
It is now eight months into the corona times;
Of lockdowns, paused lives,
Lived at subsistence level.

So many seasons have rolled into the past,
Like whistle stops,
Winter, spring, summer, rains and now autumn;
Fleeting images from the train window.

Daylight stokes fears,
But the night is calm, hiding them;
Air fragrant with frangipani blooms
The snug wrap of the dark;
Jupiter and Mars dotted above.

As if one is back into childhood;
On the threshold of life,
The veil of future still to lift;
The paths ahead still mesmerizing.

Poetry . . . The Best of 2020

Helen Campbell is from Dublin. Her work has appeared in *The Sunday Tribune* and *The Blue Nib* as well as *RTE1* and *BBC Radio 4*. She has recently completed an M.A. in Creative Writing in Dublin City University.

Encounter in Sorrento
Helen Campbell

Late for lunch, I take a turn
down a shady side street
overhung with washing lines
like ragged bunting.
Aromas of garlic, onion, oil,
hang in the stagnant heat.
Under an open window
My gaze is caught by an eye
that bulges over the rim of a dirty pail,
a bulbous head whooshes up
subsides back into scum.
A flailing tentacle seeks purchase,
succeeds - hauls up globular body.
Warty tentacles slosh filthy water
Onto the cobbles.
The amorphous blob becomes
two eyes that fix on mine,
a smiling mouth.
Transfixed
I gape at this creature
Who pulsates frantically to escape.
For a moment I believe
I could be a saviour,
grab the bucket
toss it over the wall
observe it slide gracefully into the deep.
Through the window, a racket,
voices raised, plates clattering,
knives sharpening.
The door rattles,
the moment passes. Craven,
I hurry on up the gloomy street.
They say it has a brain
can solve problems.
Not this one.

Poetry... The Best of 2020

Lovelyn P. Eyo is a multi-award winning writer from Nigeria. She is a Life Coach and an Ambassador for Peace and Cultural creativity. She was appointed Guardian of the World Union of Poets and also honored for literary excellence by the Indian government on the occasion of the country's 74th Independence Day.

Life Is Game
Lovelyn P. Eyo

Life is game
Tis not always same
It can go wild
With the need to tame
Till gets mild

It can play tricks
With a simple flick
And I am in it
With a great aim
To have my name
Under the greats of life filed
Keeping my focus
In good nick
To carve out a locus
With wisdom-bricks

Life is on
It keeps ticking
Since I- living
I will keep trying
As it goes on

The game isn't over
Not over for me
Tis only over
When GOD calls me over

I am still in it
The time still on
I am still on it
The time for me
The chance for me to win
    - continues

Tis not yet over
Because GOD-given strength
   -renews

Day after day it hovers
With blessed breath
I am still in it
I got life
I got the game
To reach my aim
I got to keep playing
Till I win
And keep winning
In this game called life

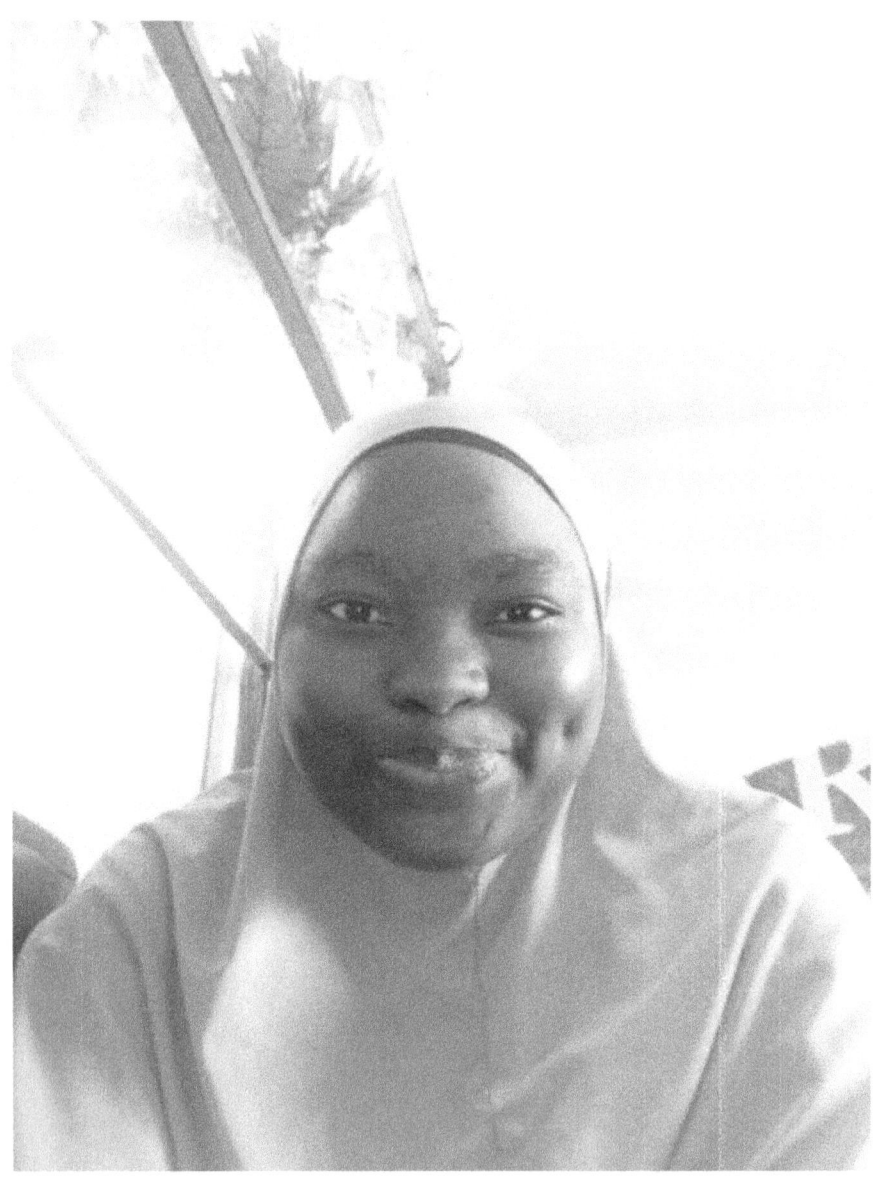

Oyewole Barakat Tobiloba is currently a student of English language in Obafemi Awolowo University. Her love for reading and productivity attract her to poetry writing. She has her poems on "The speaking heart" blog, which include "Pride, Root of all Evils", "Dead Hope" and many more.

House of Memories
Oyewole Barakat Tobiloba

This golden house has birthed many children,
But the fate of life has teared them apart –
Far from home to different destinations.
I paced through the house
& the noisy silence draws
Back my attention to those golden days:
When the rooms were scattered;
And the parlor was littered
With loads of toys,
When the house was noisy
With the children's jokes and laughter;
When the kitchen was left unkempt
& kept with piles of plates.
But now! clean & in order.
Albeit their memories, can't ever be cleaned –
They have left this house with album of pictures;
The echoes of their laughter keep
Revibrating in every angle of the rooms.

Julius Joy Oluwaseun is a sociable, smart and teachable person who is ready to unleash her potentials.

Nipped Pride
Julius Joy Oluwaseun

Like a tender rose in petals- full bloom:
Innocently dances to the rhythm of the breeze
Tender buds hums perfect melody,
The glory of the sun brings harmony,
Because I was young.

Only half a dozen age was I
Always run to Papa; graced with comfort and care,
The angry face of Mama tells spank was near,
Daily I tremble at this with fear
Because I was young.

With Papa I find solace:
Every morning with sweets and ties my lace,
No wonder he always calls me grace,
Whenever he sees my face
Because I was young.

Mama never bothered at my withdrawal;
She usually says ' Go and meet your Papa '
I was only drawn to what gave me love
Because I was young.

Papa did the unspeakable!
Took away with him my Pride and Security,
Exchanged it for affections and charity
Because I was young.

Just like every other day;
Mama never noticed I was going hay wire
I am being violated daily!
It was emotionally draining
Because I was young.

Now I am grown, in sophomore,
I still remember all in a flash back,
He does too, says tell no one
Am I a tramp not to expose Papa?
I really want freedom.

I just want to be sane,
So I can live like other bevies once again.

Poetry... The Best of 2020

Mircea Dan Duta, poet, film scientist, translator, and cultural events organizer, writes in Czech. He has authored three poetry books, *Landscapes, Flights and Dictations* (2014), *Tin Quotes, Inferiority Complexes and Human Rights* (2015), and *Please Switch off Your Mobile Phones* (2020). Some of his work has been translated into more than 20 languages.

jízdní řád
Mircea Dan Duta

vlak má deset minut zpoždění
chce se mi spát
ven už není vidět
v kupé je hrozné vedro
koukají ti kalhotky pššt to se neříká
musíš spát
vlak má dvacet minut zpoždění
klimatizace nefunguje
zkus si alespoň lehnout
nemůžeme otevřít okno jsi nachlazený
vlak má třicet minut zpoždění
na chodbě je tma
vleže na tvoje kalhotky vidím ještě líp pššt takhle nemluv
kdyby tě slyšel průvodčí tak nás vyhodí z vlaku
přece jsi mi řekla že ti nesmím nic tajit
v Blansku budeme až po půlnoci
že se před tebou nesmím vůbec skrývat
vlak má půlhodinové zpoždění
že jsi moje nejbližší bytost
čím se dostaneme domů z nádraží
že ti mám říct všechno
pojedeme taxíkem
všechno co vidím slyším cítím
to si nemůžeme dovolit
vše o čem přemýšlím
vlak má hodinu zpoždění
všechno po čem toužím
hrozně se potím mám žízeň
všechno co mě napadá
máme jenom colu a tu nesmíš
už žádné emhádéčko nejezdí
všechno co chci
vlak má tříhodinové zpoždění

hoříš máš teplotu
všechno o čem se mi zdá
už téměř všechno vidím mlhavě
ale tvoje kalhotky jsou vidět jasně
všechno co si představuju
říkala jsi vždycky že mezi námi funguje
takové intimní osvětlení jako v tom starém filmu
pšst pšst a proč stejně všichni spí
vlak má čtyřhodinové zpoždění
nikdo nevidí kam se dívám
rachot vlaku slyším jako pod vodou
to se nedělá ale říkalas že se ti mám vždycky zpovídat
musíš spát
ze všeho co nevidím neslyším necítím nechci
točí se mi hlava
o čem nepřemýšlím o čem se mi nezdá
proboha snad nezastavíme i v Adamově
po čem netoužím
ani průvodčí už nepřijde
všichni spí
mám zavráť
světla zhasla i v kupé
musíš spát
už nejsme v Adamově
ale vlak se do pohybu nedal
už nic nevidím ani tvoje kalhotky
a nevím proč
ležím přece hlavou ve tvém klíně
ještě vydržím
musíš spát
ještě nechci usnout
musím ti to říct
přece ti musím říct všechno
chci to totiž vidět
až se to stane
až vlak znovu pojede

až klimatizace začne fungovat
až se otevřou okna
až se napiju coly
až hlavou ve tvém klíně
tvoje kalhotky uvidím tak zblízka
že už nikdy neztratím zpáteční cestu
už nikdy nebudu mít zpoždění
už nikdy nezmeškám emhádéčko
už nikdy nebudu cestovat ničím jiným než tebou
budeš navždy moje emhádéčko
z tebe už nikdy nevystoupím
a žádný průvodčí mě nevyhodí
a už ti o sobě nebudu muset nic říkat

protože o mně budeš všechno vědět
stejně jako tehdy
podle jízdního řádu

timetable
Mircea Dan Duta

the train is ten minutes delayed
i want to sleep
one can no longer see anything outside
it's dreadfully hot inside
your panties peep out hush this should not be said
you have to sleep
the train is twenty minutes delayed
air-conditioning does not work
try at least to lie down
we cannot open the window you're cold
the train is thirty minutes delayed
the corridor is dark
lying down i can see your panties even better hush do not say that
if the conductor heard you he'd kick us off the train
didn't you tell me i must not withhold anything from you
we will be in blansko only after midnight
that i must not hide anything at all from you
the train has a two-hour delay
that you are my closest creature
how do we get home from the station
that i should tell you everything
we'll go by taxi
everything i see i hear i feel
we cannot afford
everything i'm thinking about
the train is an hour delayed
everything i desire
i'm sweating like crazy and thirsty
everything that occurs to me
we have only a coke and you cannot drink it
no public transport operates now
all that i want
the train is three hours delayed
you burn you have a fever
everything that i dream of
almost everything i see dimly

but your panties are clearly visible
everything i imagine
you always said that it worked between us
such intimate lighting as in that old film
hush hush and why everyone sleeps anyway
the train is four-hours delayed
no one sees where i'm looking
i hear the rumbling of the train as underwater
that's should not be done but you said i always have to confess to you
you have to sleep
everything i cannot see i do not hear i do not feel i do not want
makes my head spin
what i'm not thinking about what i'm not dreaming about
for god's sake we won't stop at adamov
what i do not wish
not even the conductor will come now
everyone sleeps
i have vertigo
the lights went out also in the compartment
you have to sleep
we are no longer in adamov
but the train did not start to move
i cannot see anything not even your panties
and i do not know why
i lie with my head in your lap
i still can resist
you have to sleep
i still do not want to fall asleep
i have to tell you
i do have to tell you everything
i do want to see it
when it happens
when the train goes again
when the air conditioning starts to work
when the windows open
when i drink coke
when my head in your lap
will see your panties so close
that i will never lose my way back

i will never be late again
i will never miss public transport
i will never travel in anything else but you
you will be my public transport forever
i will never get out of you again
and no conductor will kick me out
and i will not have to say anything about myself to you

because you'll know everything about me
just like then
according to the timetable

Translated by Tomáš Míka

Poets of the World

Priyanka Tiwari had a poetic disposition from childhood on. Her first poem was published in a newspaper when she was 8. She has written many poems in English and Hindi, some of which appeared in local newspapers and magazines. A graduate in Biotechnology, she is currently associated with HR-Organizational Psychology. [. . .]

Fire and Brimstone
Priyanka Tiwari

Ages and aeons have sung sagas of
How from verdant wombs, took birth
Civilizations great, grand and glorious
Jewels of the Crown of Mother Earth

The bequest of the wise souls of yore
Noblest of values imbibed and ingrained
The mortals, into kinship, thus knit
Humanity flourished, Grace reigned

With loving ardor, were raised
The bastions of cultural development
But none can but yield to
The Dark Angel's advancement

Our bloodlust had them smothered
Hatred triggered widespread ravage
Oh, woe! How the "civilized" heart
Made itself so unbelievably savage!

Unfettered passions, running amok
Cities turned into funeral pyres
Unbridled spread, the flames of Wrath
Unquenchable like Hell's raging fires

The steed of avarice, galloping far and wide
And trampling all that came their way
Laid brutal siege over sanity and goodwill
Bringing in, ever so often, a new Doomsday

Innumerable lives untimely snuffed out
Grieving hearts profusely ached
As Vengeance went on a gleeful rampage
Our World with darkness plagued

Battlefields soaked with sacrificial blood
Every arsenal of destruction fervently tried
While warfare "evolved" and "modernized"
Witnessing its own desecration, Humanity cried

Era to era, generation to generation
The Devil's legacy, readily handed down
Agents of Devastation, leading the way
The world in agony, their minions drown!

Wounded empires, bleeding souls
Civilizations' death-knell shall forever ring
Games of power, of malice and greed
The world, to this fate, shall surely bring!

Poetry... The Best of 2020

Colombe Mimi Leland – French for "dove of peace". The poet says, "my mother named me after a piece by Picasso done in honor of the founding of the United Nations. My poems are often about the personal crossing with the political."

The Song of Sequestering
Colombe Mimi Leland

I was reading this story,
Not a great one,
but there was a line
that struck me -
I'm in pause mode, waiting
for the next thing to happen.
Chilling at my place.
Not really thinking or initiating,
just waiting
for things to happen that require me.
Groceries running out.
Bills.
People dying.
Whatever.
I'm just waiting.
Not anxiously waiting.
Just waiting.
Breathing in. Breathing out.
Waiting.
Those also serve who sit
and wait.

Poetry... The Best of 2020

Glenn Johnson, a 69-years-old Cherokee from Tucson, Arizona, is a Sonoran Desert dweller. He graduated from the University of Arizona with a Bachelor's Degree and a major in Inter-Disciplinary Studies: Literature, Sociology, and Psychology, followed by a Master's Degree in Counseling & Guidance.

It's a Girl
Glenn Johnson

Mother's birth canal guided
Out popped your head
Hesitated
Pros and cons weighed
Decided this world to explore
Announced cry of arrival
Someone said:
It's a Girl!

Cradled arms mother
suckled
love gaze embraced
mutual bond begun
never to be forgotten
Mother entranced
Her daughter
world of sisters received
Your place in heart sealed
Declaration profound:
It's a Girl!

Diaper change
joyous wide eyes
infant glorious smile
glowing all good of life
good ever be
Pudgy arms
pudgy legs
heaven reaching
fingers nimbly playing toes
mound of life and wonder
proudly proclaims:
It's a Girl!

Where will you go?
Who will you meet?

What will you know?
What will you accomplish?
Journey of It's a Girl!

Small to tall are stories
Not all lives a fairytale
Truth must be told:
Some terrifying
All manners abuse
Crazy men's swaths of rage
ravage destruction through sisterhood
Horrific paradox:
Born of woman
Becomes tyrant of woman
Own sufferings no excuse!
Despoiling
Disrespecting
Beauty of It's A Girl!

Still good in this world
Many lives shared fulfilled
Coupled together
friendship lovers
each other hold
joy of each other's joy
Time passing
Love gathering
Husband
Father
Knowing life blest
Hearing first child's breath:
It's A Girl!

With all done and said
Must remove my mask
And speak the truth I dread:
I bare the sins of men
Begun in youth
Allowed lodging dining

Heart thieves:
Distortion of you
Disrespect
Discount

Heard you say:
Pedestal you build
I will not climb.
No goddess
Not hot
Not sexy
Fantasies contrived
Never quench
Those addicted desires.

Words I will not forget.
You said:
I will not buy
Will not accept:
You cannot live without me.
Truth:
Answer within you
yourself must find.

You profoundly questioned
My fevered romantic oaths.
You whispered:
Professed lover
Do you truly know forever?
In my body
always carried
responsibility
knowledge
my ova of forever love
Do you know?
Considered?
You carry
always carried

seeds for my forever love.
Do you know?
Considered?
The meaning:
Being with child

Ardent lover:
What if I may?
What if I may lay down?
May take you in
Do you know?
Considered?
Same as here:
A child will be born?

Truly, Creator moves in mysterious ways
Recalling your questions
shaken
awakened
reflect
Silence of meditation
Transfixed
Immersed
Visions
Again,
lungs fluid filled
nestled
floating
    You
    I
mother's ocean
bathed
warm
safe
Loved
Revelation:
Need see you true
not as I want
You are special

I know that now.
May I say:
today
day to day
hold image of you:
Many virtues
strength
spirituality
beauty
intelligence unique

When I met you:
infatuated
admired
time shared
love for you began
so did desire.

This time
It must be right
Love I offer
No delusions
Acceptance no expectation
(although wished)

In my heart.
I have learned to cradle
This inner woman
Her inner child
Swaddled ever in my heart
Promised to thrive
Never to forget:
There was a day
A blessed moment
When you entered this world
And someone said:
How wonderful!
It's A Girl!

Poetry... The Best of 2020

Ayo Ayoola-Amale, author, creative director, poet and artist, uses art forms in peace building, in developing new thinking around economic and progressive social change issues, often including poetry and the arts as a transformational vehicle to create systemic positive change.

Be Calm
Ayo Ayoola-Amale

Be calm, the calm within the storm, strengthens.
Be calm, like the unruffled deep sea.
Be a calm soul, a soul of calm, calming like the fountains of love
Be a soul of calm, calming the body and mind. Be calm.
I see god's face in a calm soul,
from a timeless springtime,
awakening a lifetime
walking in patience, meekness, and peace.
Be calm, be the still voice of calm waking to sing,
to hold true to truth for life.
Be calm, be a soul of calm gathering wondrous beauty like the heavenly sun, winds.
Be a voice that calms as the sea breeze wings.
Be a calm voice like the light's music, flourish
with a heart as million flaming flowers.
Be this mirth of paradise
touching souls, awakening the true voice.
Be calm, be a calm soul, calming.
Those kind calm were
gentle souls calm there,
Bring a sacred calm over minds,
the sacred calm of souls
Be calm, be a calm soul, calming
A calm soul, A calm in souls, putting order and purpose into life
Be calm, be a calm soul, calming
A sacred calm to be yourself, a sacred calm to be your best.
An inner calm to be most in harmony, peaceful and free
Be calm, be a calm soul calming.
Calm, so you stand still like yourself.
Be calm. Calm, the heart of light.
Be calm, be a soul of calm.
Be a calm soul, calming.
Be a sacred calm of a soul.
A sacred calm of a soul. A sacred calm of a soul. Be calm.

Smruti Ranjan Mohanty, O.F.S, son of Raj Kishore and Shantilata Mohanty, is from Padmapur, Jagatsingpur, Odisha. He writes extensively on life and its intricacies. He is a multi-lingual poet, writer and an essayist. His work appeared in various prestigious newspapers, journals, national and international magazines and anthologies across the world.

smrutiweb.wordpress.com
smrutitanuja.blogspot.com

A Look at Life-142
Smruti Ranjan Mohanty

Let me forget
Everything I have learned
Let me exhaust
All that I have earned
Let me forget
Who I am and where from
Let me come out of
All relationships and hangovers
To visualize life in its true colour

Let me begin life once more
With no past to lean upon
No future to dream for
No status to safeguard
No relations to take care

Let me get out of the cage
Where I have been long since
The social clusters
Caste, creed and colour
Religion, dogmas and superstitions
Pelf, power and accolades
To be in fresh air
Where truly breathes life
In the serene oasis

Let me forget my name and identity
To go beyond me and all
That put limits
Pride, anger and prejudice
Ego, hatred and jealousy
Let me forget history and geography

Boundaries and territories
Myths, parables and collective conscience
To look at things in proper perspective

For the first time
Let my eyes see
Ears listen and heart speak
Let reasons take a back seat
Emotions and feelings
Come out in the open
For a change
Let me be a free bird in the blue sky
To have a romance
With all that I fancy and love.

Basab Mondal, a teacher by profession, is from Kolkata. He is a bilingual poet and columnist who writes in English as well as Bengali. His poems, stories and translations have appeared in several anthologies and literary magazines. He writes to gratify his inner self, and the world around him serves as the cue.

Moments Before Committing Suicide
Basab Mondal

I try to rehearse the names, i have been called,
I remember Brutus and 'et tu Brute' reverberate,
I chant the name of Osiris, and shuffle a pack of cards,
to find if the Ace gets ticked,
I switch off my mobile, and close my eyes
to thank my true friends.

Then, I go to close the window
a rusty nail, lying nonchalantly,
cuts me open.

My silhouette dissolves
within the penumbra of things around
I can hear the dog's bark
as does my conscience
before the curtain falls.

Seena Sreevalson is a bilingual poet, editor and translator from Kerala, India. She has compiled and edited two international anthologies of English poems, *The Current* (2019) and *Global Poetry* (2020). She is the recipient of the Poonthanam Yuva Sahithya Puraskaram award.

Her Name Is Yours
Seena Sreevalson

Honey . . .
She was called.
Drop by drop
She served everyone.
Slowly her veins dried up.
No one is ashamed.
None spoke anything,
No wind, no shower reached there.
She was left alone
Bruised and swollen with hornets bites.
She strangled a sob.
Her feeble heart
Not audible enough to decipher.

Ants lined up waiting for a feast.

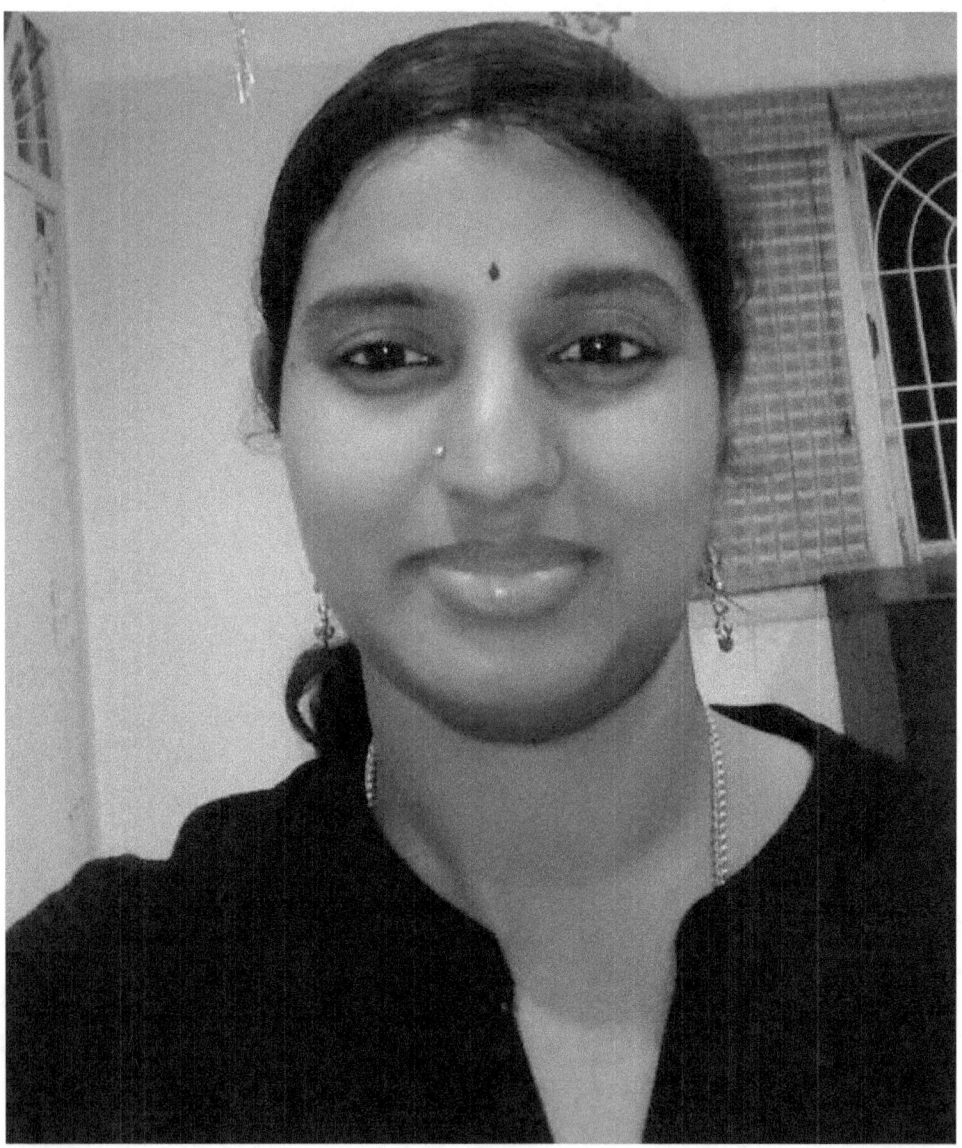

An enthusiastic story writer for children and a poet, Padmapriya Karthik holds the eighth place in the 2020 Rabindranath Tagore International Poetry Contest and received the 2020 Certificate of Excellence from the Asian Literary Society's Sagar Memorial Award. She has contributed to numerous anthologies and e-zines. Her short stories for children were published in *The PCM*.

And Away She Walks
Padmapriya Karthik

Her soul once white as cottony cloud,
Turned graphite hue
With many unshed tears.
She drifted stacking burden.
Sudden thought blow crashed.
Crippled her feet. She stood still.
Eyes drizzled cracking the rim of her burdened soul.
Tiny drops rolled down her cheek,
Up to the chin, grounded and disappeared.
Promising comfort she sensed.
She let cracks widen, poured her heart out.
Sudden gush of drops
Flushed all negate feelings and thoughts.
Soulful tears drained her burden.
And away she walks
In search of sunshine . . .

Madhumathi. H, a bilingual Indian poet and writer (Tamil and English), is an ardent lover of nature, poetry, photography and music. Her poems appeared in several anthologies and e-zines. She often writes on mental health to raise awareness and break the stigma, strongly believing in the therapeutic and transformational power of words.

madhumathi.poetry@gmail.com
https://multicoloredmoon.wordpress.com/

Prakriti – My All!
Madhumathi. H

Nature, is God's pseudonym . . .
The divine, smiles through a myriad pattern
Colors, textures, and scents of the universe
Nature nurtures, nourishes, and heals our soul
Like a doting parent, precious friend . . .
The tall brown mountains, like heaps of caramel and cocoa
The gentle wind, carrying Jasmine's whisper
Silvery streams, like flowing glass

Milky cascades, rapturous river, and the Magnum opus ocean
Nature is an artist with a magic palette
Being the canvas, and the art too
Heals our frail soul, waters our parched heart
Gently hugs our quivering tears, and
Transforms them into sunshine smiles, and laughter . . .

Love-scented oxygen from the gallery of green
Colors on petals, sticking to my soul to bloom in my dreams
Crisp blue sky, Parijat-kissed breeze
Nectar from the flowers, drenching my heart
Honeyed-joy treasured from everyday walks
Solitude, sprouting from the womb of silence
Nature heals, and restores hope . . .

Like a child my heart pauses, at
The twigs the birds use to build their nests
'A home is made of hearts', and
I hear happy conversations, when I listen to the twigs . . .
Those golden yellow blossoms, Peach, Majenta, white Bougainvillea
Gulmohar, smiling at the sparrows, and squirrels
Dreamy milky lilac, ochre leaves with crimson splashes

Half-bitten badam shell, in beetroot shades
Clutching them, my palm blushes too, while eyes grin
(Ssshhh! No! I can't share them, please . . .)
None of the blossoms I carry home were plucked but picked

As they swirl from the branches, and
Kiss the earth, sometimes
Land on the vehicles that hibernate . . .

Pebbles, from the riverside walk
Myriad leaves as fabrics of seasons
The eucalyptus, soul's aroma therapy
Oranges and lemon, intoxicating
Pomegranates and mangoes, appetizing
Deliciousness abound, in Nature's world . . .
Some feathers are the resume of birds
That carry stories of faraway Skies, and restored answers
Reminding me, Nature is my nest, home, cradle and swing . . .

My Mitr Mentor shoulder and anchor, Nature
Asks me to believe each day
I belong to those emerald feathers
Sunshine petals, Azure blue of the canopying sky, and
To a million hues of the universe
Its eternal patterns, and
My soul camouflaged by Nature
Am an obedient student, surrendering to Nature's immortal feet
Observing with love, allowing myself to be absorbed . . .

Can I ever stop, from sharing
What all my soul inhales in rapture, but
Somewhere I have to, while Nature
Will be gifting me bliss each day
Sunsets and moon rises, butterflies bird songs to thunder
Rhythm of rain, Petrichor, clouds and the taste of raindrops . . .
Each day, my heart would expand and explode in joy
Stacking up the treasures from Nature . . .
At the break of dawn
As a dewdrop kisses a blade of grass, and the earth melts

A brand new heart, gets ready
For all the Euphoria!
I elope with Nature every single day, and
Come back home, with a blushing soul

Poetry... The Best of 2020

A healed heart, stolen kisses from the flowers, and
A mind as light as mist
Like Wordsworth, Keats, Bharathi, and Shelley
Nature never did betray me
My last breath will smell of gratitude and love, settling on eternity's lake
Please meet me in my poems, for
My soul shall never leave my words
That Metamorphose as Nature . . .

*Prakriti (Sanskrit): "nature"; Badam: "almond"; Parijat: Indian night-flowering coral jasmine – a fragrant flower; Mitr: "friend"; Bharathi, "Mahakavi" Subramania Bharathi, was a Tamil writer, poet, journalist, an Indian independence activist, a social reformer and a polyglot. He was a pioneer of modern Tamil poetry and is considered one of the greatest Tamil literary figures of all time.

Orbindu Ganga is an Indian science post-graduate and the first recipient of Dr. Mitra Augustine Gold Medal for Academic Excellence. He is the founding director of the English literary journal, *INNSÆI*, author, poet, content writer, painter, researcher, and spiritual healer. He has published many poems, research papers, articles, and has a painting.

Verisimilitude of Self
Orbindu Ganga

Acceptance

Clouds were hovering
Around the mountain,
Waiting for the time
To sprinkle the drops,
Patiently looking
At the cumulus
To give a glance,
Never did he realize
The time was
Never his master,
Never did the time
Gave him the hint,
Being dry for ages
He pleaded the time
For respite knowing
His act of kindness,
Moving away from
The thought to think,
He obeyed the norms
To cleave the weeds
Seeing within him
Accepting the flow.

Realization

Fine drizzle captured
The essence of being,
Seeing the mizzle
The realization to kiss
The drizzle ricocheted,
Waiting for the mizzle to
Mist into the drizzle,
The wait has become
Longer than ever before,

Poets of the World

Testing the curves within
Patience was watching
Silently along the lane,
Mizzle drained into
Finer fragments,
Giving the drizzle
The thought to whisper,
Looking into her for long
She left the traces,
Kissing the drops
Realizing the essence.

Uncondition

Vacuoles were opened
To see the outside world,
To be empty never
Gave them the solace,
Being emptied never
Was the sign of zilch,
Being living as vacuoles
For the eternity was
The assumption
To be amarantine,
Conditioned for generations
Never had an iota of thought
To stop the belief
To stop the emotion
To stop living,
Did the thought surfaced
Deep one day to take
The decision
To uncondition the form
To cleave the existing
To begin from nought.

Unknown

To have layered

The ricocheted thoughts
Leave from the sight,
The traces were
Finding the absence
With the presence
Of the unknown,
The existing is absent
With the beginning
To nullify the presence,
Absence is the beginning
For the presence to
Start from the unknown,
Unconditioned plane
Is left with thoughtlessness
For the nothingness
To thrive leaving
Everything behind.

Flowing

The new beginning
Without a thought
Is the presence
Of the absence,
To let nothingness
Stay still in the flow
Of the absence,
The formless being
Shall exist for eternity
In search of the truth
To know the self.

Anwesha Paul is a UX designer and graphic artist from Kolkata, India who is also into writing, having contributed to various print and online publications. Anwesha is an animation filmmaker whose short films have been screened and awarded in various international film festivals.

Death and Deathlessness
Anwesha Paul

The wordless poem
The formless painting
The soundless song
The bottomless pit
The emptiness which defies definition
The crucible of dissolution.

Ah! The freedom of being ness
The awareness of nothingness
Watching the waves of creation
Crash into the shores of non-existence,
If this is death, then let me die to every moment
For I AM.

Annapurna Sharma A. is Deputy Chief Editor of Muse India (www.museindia.com) and writes the column Life & Literature for the Muse India journal. Her works are forthcoming, or have appeared, among others, in *Westward Quarterly*, *Mad Swirl*, *Spark*, *Destine Literare*, *Reader's Digest*, *Women's Era*, *Assam Tribune*, and *Active Muse*.

I Long to Sing You a Summer Song . . .
Annapurna Sharma A.

Resting in the shade of Babul
I await your return
the quietness of your footsteps
the mellowness of your being

When you set out, the sun was bleeding
redness from your veins
limping across the bone-dry landscape
you fetch three pitchers of water
(one for me, two for your folks)

I long to sing you a summer song
melding your ossified heart
I desire to write endless poetries
with the cracks in your feet and
aches in your arms

I yearn to become the Prince of your dreams:
unleashing my energies to dig a well in your backyard
and threaten the sun crossing line at 50

I crave to plant orchids in your parched courtyard
and rein the sand dunes from rolling over your cheeks
sprinkling yellows of Babul on the roof
licking echoes of contorted tongues
driving away the perfidious creature in your bed . . .

This birth: I repay your summer love,
in naked winter, with my fleece

You splash blue from your dupatta
onto the dead skies of Churu
into the silent waters . . .

I wish to be re-born
as a verse from your womb

Dr. Queen Sarkar is a multilingual poet, an academician, a reviewer and translator working as an Assistant Professor in the University Department of English, Ranchi University. She is an Academic counselor in IGNOU. Sarkar has a Ph.D. from IIT. Her review articles, poems, and research papers have been published internationally.

Battle
Dr. Queen Sarkar

Demeaning stereotypes and labels,
breaking portraits of delusional battles,
I stand firm,
to voice against the brazen misogynistic rattle.

Wading through the mysterious brook of hope I heal,
transforming my pain into power,
I refuse to kneel.

Messy hormonal results, sometimes,
undesired 9 months struggle,
I chose to break taboos,
fighting till I create my own world,
which can't be deliberately misconstrued and barreled.

Adesunwon Babatunde Habideen, from Lagos State, Nigeria, is an undergraduate student at Obafemi Awolowo University, Ile Ife, Osun. He is studying Education and Political Science. He is also a poet who loves teaching and writing poems and expresses his concerns and thoughts through poetry.

Birth Day
Adesunwon Babatunde Habideen

The beautiful heart full of blessings
Trinity entail with mercy
Shining ideas of love, truth and joy,
Filled our mouth with joy.

Mother blessed our days with adage;
Father bathed us with courage.
Beautifying our days with essence,
Which we crave for his presence.

Yesterday was the day you're born;
Today we celebrate you at one;
Igniting you to our Parenthood.
Filled with responsibility and price yet decision are made aboard.

Even with so much thought and laws;
Here lies the happy hours of ours,
When mother drives us safely to world,
And father welcomes us with his word.

A happy moments of joy,
Filled with laughter and love.
Incision of praise and worship,
Dawn with his welcome of lordship.

Poets of the World

Zana Coven, born in Sarajevo (former Yugoslavia), resides in Italy. She writes poetry, short stories, travel diaries and haiku. She has authored 4 books. Her work has appeared in numerous international publications. She is the recipient of a large number of awards. In 2019, she received the unique award of Italian poetry critics in Milano, Italy.

Too Tired
Zana Coven

Is this end of the world
Or just warning of how small
We are thinking we can all
We believed we were gods
Having under control
we see and what
We cannot see
Changing the rules of nature
Changing the normal going of things
That not belong to us
We thought we are immortal
By changing our faces
But all we achieve is a new
Fake and artificial life

Is this the punishment
We deserved with our greed
Thinking some are better
Or we wanted to combat somebody
Making weapons that are
Smarter than us
And return to us as boomerangs
We pay with the only thing we have
Our lives sacrificed to our nonsense
Empty of goodness
Full of selfishness

Our souls, what is with our souls
I feel as I lived for centuries
Too old , too tired, too sick
Empty soul, broken in sadness
The old soul

That saw the worst, believing in the best
And living like
I am in a waiting room
Waiting for mankind
To change!

Poetry... The Best of 2020

Tejaswini Patil, academic, poet, editor and social worker, is the founding director of *Innsæi*. She writes about nature, social issues, and feminist sensibilities. She has authored four collections of poetry (published by Boundless, USA), was included in 25 Women of Virtue, and has been awarded the Master of Creative Impulse prize.

Leaf and the Window-pane
Tejaswini Patil

All windows of my abode
Open towards rain . . .
The gusts bring with them
A colourful unperished leaf
Floating from Fall.
It's stuck on the window-pane
Facing me.
Drowned in its colours, I float back
To its origin
Passing through seasons.
At certain time,
I'm stuck in.
Why did it come to me?
How did it reach me?
Why didn't it wither ?
Was it searching for
a fellow sufferer . . .?
Now, I sail on the winds
Like that leaf of foliage
Searching for another window-pane.

Bozena Helena Mazur-Nowak, a Pole, resides in the UK since 2004. She has authored seven poetry collections. Her work may be found in more than 100 anthologies and magazines worldwide. She won numerous poetry competitions. Her poetry has been translated into 20 languages.

It Might Be the Last Lesson
Bozena Helena Mazur-Nowak

just yesterday they believed it would be okay
they fought for every breath, for every sip of life
today rows of only empty chairs remind of them,
the cat mewing in the armchair and dog in tears

loved ones should be close, but they were so far away
there was no one to hold their hands and tightly hug
now they lay lonely in rows of nameless coffins
in the middle of nowhere waiting for the grave

where did it all start and how it happened, who knows?
they say in China but are they really sure?
if there would not be the pursuit of money and power
there would not be so many hungry people in the world

there is enough money for bombs and space rockets
the food drowns in the sea by some madmen creatures
and their sick visions instead of feeding the hungry
although tomorrow, our world may cease to exist

it is still not too late to shake off the madness
to learn from this cruel and maybe last warning
first of all, people must be treated equally
the rest will slowly follow when you open your heart

Jyotirmaya Thakur, a retired Principal, has authored 23 books with more waiting to be published and translated into 57 languages [. . .]. She translates Hindi for the *ITHACA* magazine of Spain. Reviewer, columnist, editor, academic, motivational speaker, philanthropist, and spiritual and social activist, she has received multiple awards.

Inner Peace
Jyotirmaya Thakur

A peaceful day is so hard to find
When communication is unkind
Commotion of others greed you find
Infects your life with their corrupt mind.

You hear the wind whistle in your ears
Closing your eyes you lose all fears
Nothing is permanent you are sure
This rays of hope makes it clear.

Sitting with serenity near riverside
Waves crash into rocks mesmerized
The cool breeze just calms my soul
And guides me towards life's goal.

Sun shines through the grey clouds
Golden halo around makes me proud
I can feel God's grace draws near
I feel the beauty of moment here .

The soothing twilight slowly brings
An astonishing reality of sights
Running wild after material things
Is such a waste of sleepless nights.

I want right now to just go slow
And let time go by as life will flow
It's on days like these I truly treasure
Amazing moments of beautiful weather.

I wonder and feel like life is a bliss
The day draws near your worries cease
It's enough for me to fade into the night
Tranquility I feel helps me win the fight.

Ashok Kumar is a bilingual mystical poet from India. He is a principal in a reputed institution in India. He is an international peace activist. He believes in the philosophy of Dr. Nelson Mandela, R. N. Tagore and Gandhian thoughts. His poems have been translated into various languages, such as Greek, Spanish and Russian.

[sic] No Title
Ashok Kumar

Let me be a child,
with wishes and care
Not to be rich and renowned
Let us bear the pain
Listen the voice of the rain
Vices and hypocrisy
reside in the fame
Humble heart has no place
for hate
Simplicity, generosity can
change the fate
None can hold time
be man of word to shine
let's love all colours
to live valuable life
let's think which left us behind
Come, walk hand in hand
for mankind
let's not claim for superiority
every heart has inner beauty
let me be the preacher
of equality
the earth is a beautiful place
to attain spirituality
Let's be universal soul
 to reach our humanity goal
Let's be fearless,
stand firmly suffer heroically
for our nations
Love and hope should be
our passions
be true, sincere soul of his creation

Olaifa Omodolapo Roseline is a Nigerian poet who through her writings has brought healings to the wounded and the voice to the voiceless.

Di-vorce
Olaifa Omodolapo Roseline

We were so much attached to each other
I couldn't sleep without your thought roaming in my head as i was your heartbeat.

What happened?
Did you listen to what they say?
They do not want our happiness
Do you not know?

Do you want our story to be like that of Lagbaja?

But why?

Do you want our story to be told like that of Tàmédo?

Oh! Ife mi
So soon you've forgotten . . . You told me i look like Yemonja, the river goddess
and I'll born you generations of nations.

Your promises were yay and now, nay.
I still keep mine and clinches to them like the lizard on the wall.

You told me no death for us because love never dies and if it comes,
We'll walk hand in hand to our maker

Have you not remembered?
You told me you would love me till the end
Come what may,
But this is not the end
And we're still in May.

Suddenly,
You dislike my taste
And throw me away like waste
My presence disgust you
Like used sawdust

If it is fate,
I'll carry on with faith

Feel free to pressure me at your leisure
I'll carry on with the seizure.

I may fall ill
But will get healed.

Mahmoud Said Kawash, born in Palestine, resides in Denmark. A poet, writer and researcher, he holds two degrees in management and literature with experience in the fields of higher education, translation and written and audio media. He served as the director of an Arabic-speaking radio, and authored three books in politics and literature.

kawashmahmoud@yahoo.co.uk

Eve, the Great!
Mahmoud Said Kawash

(Dedicated to my youngest sister Rajaa who has just finished treatment from the cancer. May Allah bless her and her family!)

Eve is Great
How great she is
Yes, she is great
And the secret of her greatness is in her motherhood
In her tenderness, kindness and femininity
And in everything she has and does

Eve amazes me
Yes, she amazes me
She amazes me by attending her enduring passion
She is the first to express her love and show sympathy
She is the first to smile and to shed tears
And often her smiles and tears mix together

She is the first to show tenderness
To experience her tenderness, try when you are sick
Or pretend to be sick
Try and get sick
Then you will see her fear for you
And feel when she wipes your head with her warm hand
Her hand is always warm!!

If you get sick and your temperature becomes high
Ask Eve to put her hand on your forehead
You will feel it's warmer than your forehead!!
How can this be when your temperature is high?
It is an amazing secret
Eve's warmth does not emit from her blood as is the case for us
Rather, it always rushes from the warmth of her present emotion!!

You see Eve asleep and her hand on her baby
How to do that while she is sleeping?
Doesn't she move her hand with feeling, as we do?

It seems that Eve does not sleep at all
Rather, her passion always remains awake
She is always alert and ready

You can put your head on her shoulder whenever you like
Even if she is angry with you
Put your head on her shoulder
You find her hand wiping your head automatically
Wonderful!!
Why can't you do that?

Really, Eve is amazing
No wonder God "Almighty" made her deserve the best company
No wonder He made Paradise under her feet
Amazing is Eve
And great is she
And great is Adam when he reads her better!!

Greetings and appreciation to you, dear Eve
You are the mother, the sister, the wife and the daughter
The auntie and the aunt
The Sweetie and the girlfriend
It is you whom "Prophet of Mercy" said: "Have pity on her"
The Holy Prophet is truthful

Greetings and appreciation to you Eve,
Everywhere and anytime
Every moment and with every whisper!!
May Allah bless you
You are really great
How great you are Eve!!

Keisha Ballentyne is a talented entrepreneur who is inspired by "Lifting Spirits Poetically" – the slogan for her poetry. She bases her poems on the reality of individuals' daily lives by connecting to them mentally, spiritually and emotionally. [. . .] She has over 30 audience-engaging poems, and currently works on having them published.

Is It About the Color of My Skin or Is It the Melanin?
Keisha Ballentyne

From a thousand miles yet moments entwined,
I'm drenched in your copious, Heavenly sweet high notes of tranquility,
yet fierce gravity that only you have the Sovereignty and authority to unfold the captivity
of my sacred soul . . .

The realms of my spirit are greatly under
attack at this very moment . . .
"Is it about the color of my skin?" "Or is it the Melanin?"
Dry times seeps it's way through a hollow crack . . .
The perpetual hills that I tried so hard to escape bows at your feet.

So then tell me, why do my adversaries
gang up on me like a pack of wolves?
"Is it about the color of my skin?" "Or is it the Melanin?"
Why so often am I pushed aside, disregarded and hated?

Am I too special, exceedingly gifted, yet humble
before your presence . . . Are we not from One God?
One world? One race? One love? . . . Black Kings!
Black Queens! Rise!! Emancipate your mind from mental slavery.

Elohim, Adonai The great I am is within.

NRK Srikar has several poems on varied themes in English, some of which appeared in national and international anthologies. He likes participating in online contests. An ardent lover of nature and avid reader, his interests include photography, exploring technology, and drawing sketches. Presently, he is an Associate Consultant in Atos|Syntel, Pune.

norisrikar@gmail.com

The Dance of the Night Beauty
NRK Srikar

The most mystifying of God's creation
Preaches many exciting things in action
Revelation of darkness always inspires
Concealment of facts equally conspires
It's the beautiful trait of the dark night!!

Many a nocturnal being deem it cordial
They come out and operate in congenial
The sea redoubles its beauty in the night
The waves dancing to the echoes upright
It's the fabulous dance of the dark night!!

The night lady clad in black robes glistens
The necklace of silver stars forms margins
The plait of milky-way with bright garnish
All planets as circlet of flowers embellish
It's the striking charm of the dark night!!

The enthralling silver-spread pleasant place
Fills the exhausted mind with cheery grace
Moving along the white frothy waves rolling
A sudden meteor shines as the nice nose pin
It's the cute twinkling soul of the dark night!!

The five elements as scented mystic bowers
Tinkling hum by pebbles in melodic waters
Cool breezes waft pleasant thoughts hearty
Fills the ambiance with sweet scenic beauty
It's the exceptional taste of the dark night!!

The luring musical notes of Nature's song
In all varied manifestation across and along
The divine dance of night beauty's elegance
At the Universal garden of divine entrance
It's the celestial wonder of the dark night!!

Shoma Bhowmick, regional director of Suryadaya Literary Foundation, was featured among 350 "Year's" writers across the world and has received an award from the Gujarat Sahitya Akademi [. . .]. She is an educator who resides in Kolkata, and is in the advisory board of *Namaste Ink*. She was awarded numerous prestigious prizes [. . .].

Humanity
Shoma Bhowmick

Be a lotus in the
Filth and dirty water of life
Else diamond in the
Dark and dirty coal mine.

Be a mountain when
The cyclone come
In all odds
Maintain your decorum.

Like the majestic rain
Clean all your surroundings
In case of new relationship
Don't forget your old bondings.

It is better to stand
Bare feet
Than to borrow
Else's boot.

Like a banyan tree
Don't forget your root.

Abhilipsa Kuanar, a budding dentist [. . .], is a poet, an avid reader and a literature enthusiast. Her poems reflect her sensitivity, emotions and [. . .] life experiences. [. . .] What else can a poet dream for, other than her poems in the people's heart and mind all over the world?

abhilipsakuanar@gmail.com

The Fragility of Life
Abhilipsa Kuanar

Inhaling the memory of
Smirked summer
I remember
How naively I accepted slavery
To sleep yesteryear

I cupped my malar
With fingers tender
Didn't dance to the rain
Only to realise later
We don't get chances so often

The desires or
Better referred
Despair
Agiled through my body
Just to wane me faster

Now I walk past an expanse
Of few meters
Expecting bounty
Earlier through the harsh roads
I merrily suffered,
With the forethought of plenty

The road never ended
And here I am
All tired, realized
How I wasted all my years
In the pursuit of nothing
All my wishes battered

Poetry... The Best of 2020

Remorse running in my sleeves
Dandelions crashing choir
Gaily yet cold heartedly
I pretend and play parts
But none mine

More my heart aches
More I put the stones of melancholy
On the ruins of my youth
I play my favourite memory.

Shiv Raj Pradhan is a Gandhian poet and social activist. His poems have appeared in about 12 English and Spanish anthologies. Numerous national and international poetry organizations have honoured his work with accolades and certificates. He is a World Record Attempter and possesses World Record Certificates.

I Will Ever Call You!
Shiv Raj Pradhan

I will call you, believe me, in a part of drumming cheer
By contending riddle stripped bed etched in an inch ere
Believe me, I'll call you, over dabbling track of absurd affair
By consistently standing against score of hysteric blare.

Alluding trumpet text from dream of disillusioned alley
Piling up muse surge from debris of debauched sway
Hoarding smile acreage from sob note of wounded day
Believe me, I'll call you, by cheering chant of soul, all on way.

Rolling by knee part through cone of bulged insipid ridge
Faltering but steadily wielding kink of pulse by tricky hit
Righting the dauntless chant yet timing with brisk tweet
Even in ruined stage at lone lane, I'll call you in verse sweet

I'll call you, believe me, by waking up from stages of debacle
Beckoning to lively lap of dream rush from core of fresh tale
Resetting tumbling placidity of yours, to rhythmical sail
At shaky dawn, toiling thru bouts, believe me, I'll quote my call.

Poets of the World

Michelle Joan Barulich enjoys writing poetry and songs. She loves [. . .] animals, and has rescued birds – her pets now, bringing her much happiness. She studied Alternative Medicine [. . .] and is a part-time caregiver. Her interests include art, calligraphy, and wood-burning. She aspires to become a licensed wildlife rehabilitator.

Make a Memory for Me
Michelle Joan Barulich

. . . Born on a snow flowing day
They make a destiny for us to rely upon
But nothing matters if you're not with me
And they can't change that

. . . In the sunlight, moonlight
The weather catches my smile
Dazzling with gold and silver
The memory comes alive

Today, the wind is pushing east
Trying hard to tell you
The thoughts that I felt
When we kissed

In the candle light, dim-lit
Shadows covered us whole
I guess what I'm trying to say is
Make a memory for me
so when time passes
I can at least say
some parts of life were good

Make a memory for me
And I'll make a memory for you
In the lime light, ultralight
You can say I was the one
Who made you complete

Six years if still no approval
Where would my future take me?
well come on now,
I need your exchange of words

Poets of the World

In the highlight, firelight
Our souls burned as one
Make a memory for me
And I'll sing you a song

. . . In the sunlight, moonlight
The Heavens were kind
Shimmering with china white stars
The memory comes alive once again . . .

Poetry... The Best of 2020

D.L. Lang served as the poet laureate of Vallejo, California (2017-2019). She has performed hundreds of times since 2015 at protest rallies, county fairs, and literary events. She has authored 13 poetry books poetry and the editor of Verses, Voices, and Visions of Vallejo. Find her online at poetryebook.com

Goals for a New Year
D. L. Lang

This year I will accept myself.
This year I will love myself.
This year I will recognize
that I did my best.

This year I will choose a new direction.
This year I will abandon unhealthy habits.
This year I will follow my inner voice.
This year I will put my needs first.

This year I will apologize to myself
for all the previous years
when I did not center my wellbeing.
This year I will forgive myself.
This year I will abstain from guilt.
This year I will let go of shame.

This year I will not seek perfection.
This year my shortcomings
will not outweigh my successes.
This year I will revel in gratitude.
This year is my year to shine!

Poetry... The Best of 2020

Hema Ravi is a poet, reviewer, an author, editor (*Efflorescence*) and independent researcher. Her writings have been featured in several online and international print journals, a few have won prizes. In July 2020, she has organized an international poetry webinar, "Connecting Across Borders". She is a freelancer for IELTS & Communicative English.

Hit the Bull's Eye

Aim high! with the wind at your back, achieve your goal,
past doldrums gain momentum: achieve your goal.

Explore paths not taken, carve a niche for yourself,
serve as beacon of the oppressed, achieve your goal.

Wending along the earth's orbit, reach all corners,
leave no stone unturned in the quest - achieve your goal.

Lift the veil of selfishness to empower hearts
with enchanting words, conquer and achieve your goal.

Travel past prejudices with clear reasoning,
wading through all calamities, achieve your goal.

When winds of change usher in joys, move with caution,
sail progressively with the tide, achieve your goal.

As destination arrives, *Ma, stay on with poise,
in others' victory see yours. Achieve your goal!

*Ma: pen name of author

hülya n. yılmaz [sic] is Professor Emerita (PSU, USA), ICPI Co-Chair and Director of Editing Services, tri-lingual writer, and literary translator. She has authored five poetry books and co-authored another. Numerous anthologies of global endeavors featured her work. hülya finds it vital for everyone to understand a deeper sense of self, and writes creatively to attain a comprehensive awareness for humanity.

https://hulyanyilmaz.com

lost . . . or?
hülya n. yılmaz

people
in every corner of the fountain-square
some seating is available close-by
we walk toward one left-out spot
and sit down in our wonderous awe
under the watchful faces' curious eyes
accompanied by what i assume to be
a traditional Moroccan drum tune
mesmerizing the clear night-sky
competing with the vibrant Arabic sounds
that rise higher and higher up
from countless chats
of those for us-undecodable voices

i want to dance to the enticing rhythm
but i know this place is not mine to claim . . .

many families are promenading
with their older children
minding the safe navigations
of their little ones' toddler-go-carts
those beautiful small darlings
are grinning from ear to ear
overjoyed with their driving skills
while they keep an eye on the passers-by
their age-alike counterparts, that is
who travel around the plaza
donning many different car models
of a variety of colors and sizes
in that enviable-even-by adults
modern day-invention

one blond boy
about 2 years old
discovers the fun of obstacle-jumping
he steps his cute little feet atop a brick

Poetry... The Best of 2020

among many that shelter a healthy tree
he jumps down from it
onto the plaza's floor-concrete
while his parents talk eagerly on a bench

no boo boos
none whatsoever
he is so elated by his daring stunt
that he repeats the same in reverse
tummy-laughing in audible giggles

young couples also pass by
some glance at us in subdued demeanors
others stare bluntly and persistently
we smile and mind our own business

there are many boys of different ages
they play all kinds of outdoor games
with their fathers or with each other
girls strut their perhaps-newly-learned
steps of awakening-femininity
they look left, then right, then left again
assessing on a scale of their own making
the attention they get from the opposite sex

an almost deflated ball seems to be
the biggest attraction for some of the boys
several of them don complete soccer uniforms
with barely-worn out shoes to match
others among their team members
stand out with their everyday clothes
they make a serious effort
to keep their bathroom slippers in place

one older boy
joins the game with overt enthusiasm
he is wearing a traditional male Hijab
quite a talent this young man is

Poets of the World

with all his rapid feet-moves and leg twists
despite his neck-to-ankle-length-garb

nearest to our seats
two women-groups gather up
they sit in opposite ends
from one another
but their focus of interest
appears to be the same: gossip
their mimics and gestures are universal
descriptions of female bodies and faces
via finger-and-face-adjustments
along with the uniquely fiery octaves
of their voices, which yield to
a large variety of enunciations
flavored with laughter as well as snorts
a sign-language of disapproval? aplenty!

the same drum-tune enters the open-air again
the performers' break must be over

i want to dance to the enticing rhythm
but i know this place is not mine to claim . . .

yet, i am made to feel as if it were

wherever i went and stayed this summer
a sense of belonging has been gifted to me
in . . .

                                 Bethlehem
                                 Ramallah
                                 Amman
                                 Madaba
                                 Jericho
                                 Cairo
                                 Giza
                                 Kenitra
                                 Larache
                                 Assilah

Poetry... The Best of 2020

Monastir
Rahovec
Prizren
Skopje
Strumica

i was embraced by the ultimate warmth of loving hearts
all the dearest souls in these parts of the globe
have abundantly demonstrated to me
as to why their acts of hospitality
oozing from their hometowns
and cultural entities at large
have long ago attained
their worldwide fame

William S. Peters, Sr., aka 'Just Bill', is an award-winning global activist for humanity. His poetry and prowess have been acknowledged and translated across the world. He is the founder and chair of Inner Child Enterprises, Inner Child Press International and the World Healing, World Peace Foundation. He utilizes these vehicles along with his poetry and other writings to champion the cause of consciousness, peace, love, acceptance and compassion. His personal perspective is that 'life is a garden', and we must plant seeds of good intent, light and love that we all may harvest a sweet bountiful fruit. The 'by-line' Mr. Peters has coined for Inner Child Press International is 'building bridges of cultural understanding'. Achieving this vital connection is his inspiration.

To Laugh Again

It has been some time
Since I have laughed
With the abandon
I now embrace

The lunacy of the times
The absence of human rhymes
The lemons with the limes
Have given rise
As I surmise
All the things
We now say,
Conceive,
And believe

My laughter is the sugar
That makes all the nonsense
And the absence of sense
Palatable,
Yet never digestible

Isn't it all just one pisser?

I remember as a kid
When my father tickled me
Incessantly
Because it brought us both
A certain joy,
Much like how I am tickled now
By the things
That come from the mouth
Of babes of consciousness
And fools

The word tools they employ
To divide us from our joy
Is no coy coincidence

Poets of the World

As fences are erected
At the borders
Of our reason

The diseased season
Is upon us,
Where trust
Is a questionable paradigm
Much like those raw limes
I mentioned earlier

So, I laugh
That I may not be consumed
By the rhetoric
And misdirection,
The inflection
The selections
That beg for correction
Of the narratives

That is OK for some,
The ignorant and the plain dumb
But my friend,
We must
Learn to laugh
And alter the collective sum
With a light of insight
That is your own,
Seek out what is known
Not the poisonous seeds
That are sown
Seek . . .
And LEARN
To laugh again!

Epilogue

Inner Child Press International

'building bridges of cultural understanding'

www.innerchildpress.com

About Inner Child Press International

The U.S.-based Inner Child Press was founded in May, 2011 by William S. Peters, Sr. as a subsidiary of Inner Child Enterprises. The founder already had an extensive experience when his writings and publications are concerned. Mr. Peters' first book went into print without his awareness in 1972. In 2008, he self-published a collection of his own poems, *My Inner Garden*. Inner Child Press grew out of his desire to self-publish his own literary work, which subsequently led to assisting other writers in the publishing process.

From its early years on, Mr. Peters' writer-oriented vision and his staff of established writers have been embraced by novice authors as well as those who had been previously published. Inner Child Press has diligently preserved its original mission – writers for writers – as it grew into a globally distinguished publishing company, starting in September, 2011. A poetry contest resulted in the first edition of *World Healing World Peace* (published in April 2012). The call for submission was open to poets from all over the world. This anthology was a significant first step for the company to enter the paradigm of international recognition.

As time progressed and Inner Child Press began to publish more authors across the globe – individually and in anthologies, its international presence expanded. This growth also led to Mr. Peters and other board members making appearances at international poetry festivals, to include Kosovo, Macedonia, Lebanon, Morocco, Tunisia, Jordan, Palestine, and Canada. They also made multiple appearances across the United States. The founder's visionary tutelage, along with the company's dedicated board members, thus enabled Inner Child Press a formidable international image which led to Inner Child Press International.

Inner Child Press International, ICPI, is an integral instrument to empower the voices of writers from all regions of the world through literature and strives to leave an essential footnote in the history of humanity. William S. Peters, Sr. and everyone at Inner Child Press International envision that literature, especially poetry, possesses a unique ability to bring people together. ICPI is very adamant with its stance and has therefore appointed cultural ambassadors from every region of our world. This all-inclusive approach epitomizes the company's motto, 'building bridges of cultural understanding'.

Thank you.

Inner Child Press International

'building bridges of cultural understanding'

Inner Child Press International

'building bridges of cultural understanding'

Meet the Board of Directors

William S. Peters, Sr.
Chair Person
Founder
Inner Child Enterprises
Inner Child Press

Hülya N Yılmaz
Director
Editing Services
Co-Chair Person

Fahredin B. Shehu
Director
Cultural Affairs

Elizabeth E. Castillo
Director
Recording Secretary

De'Andre Hawthorne
Director
Performance Poetry

Gail Weston Shazor
Director
Anthologies

Kimberly Burnham
Director
Cultural Ambassador
Pacific Northwest
USA

Ashok K. Bhargava
Director
WIN Awards

Deborah Smart
Director
Publicity
Marketing

www.innerchildpress.com

Other

Socially Important Anthologies

by

Inner Child Press International

Inner Child Press Anthologies

Advisory Board
World Healing, World Peace Foundation
human beings for humanity

worldhealingworldpeacefoundation.org

Inner Child Press Anthologies

Inner Child Press Anthologies

World Healing World Peace 2020

Poets for Humanity

Now Available at
www.innerchildpress.com

Inner Child Press Anthologies

the Heart of a Poet

words for a better tomorrow

The Conscious Poets

Now Available

www.innerchildpress.com

Inner Child Press Anthologies

Now Available
www.innerchildpress.com

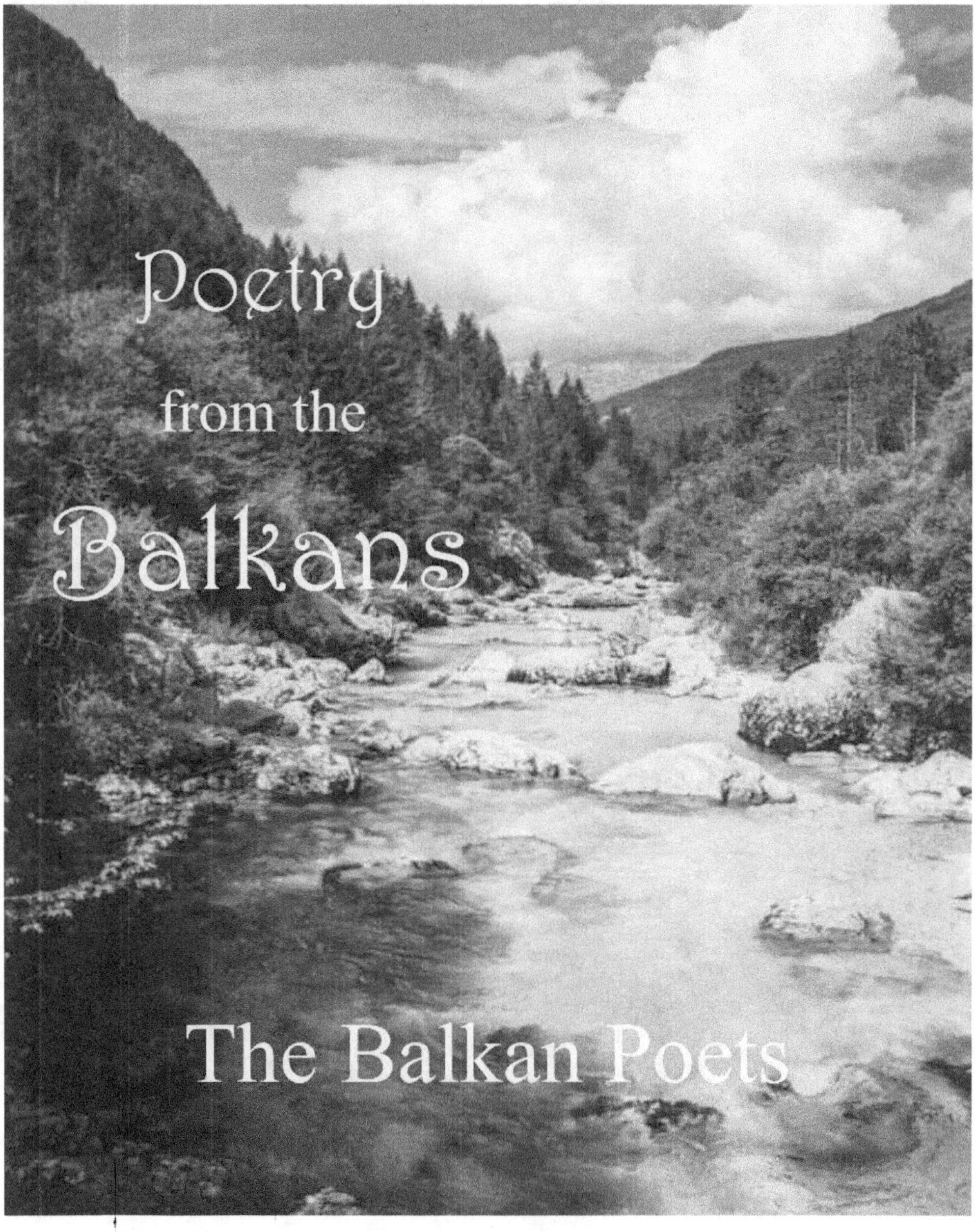

Inner Child Press Anthologies

Poetry from the Balkans

The Balkan Poets

Now Available at
www.innerchildpress.com

Inner Child Press Anthologies

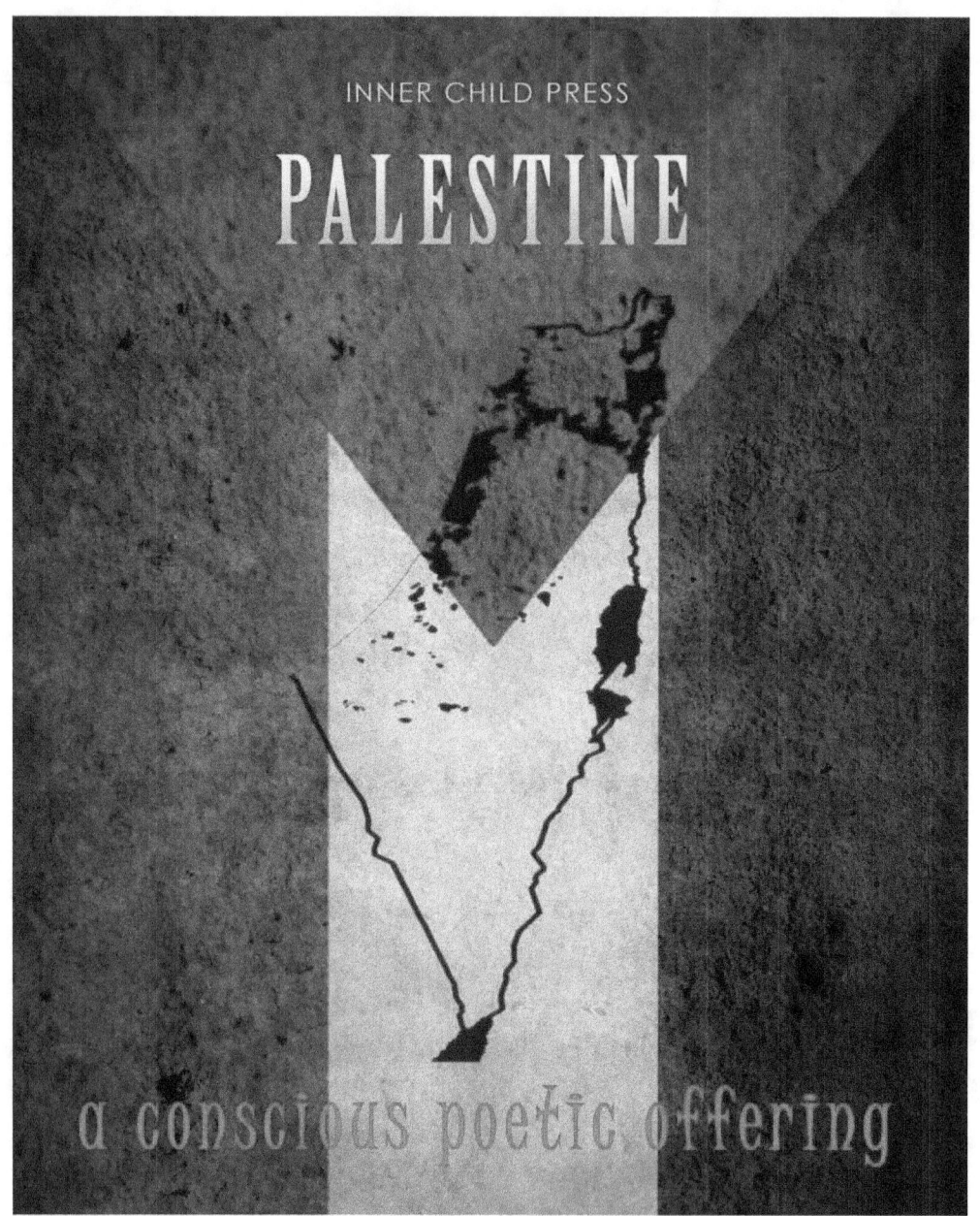

Now Available at

www.innerchildpress.com

Inner Child Press Anthologies

Now Available at
www.innerchildpress.com

Inner Child Press Anthologies

Now Available at

www.innerchildpress.com

Inner Child Press Anthologies

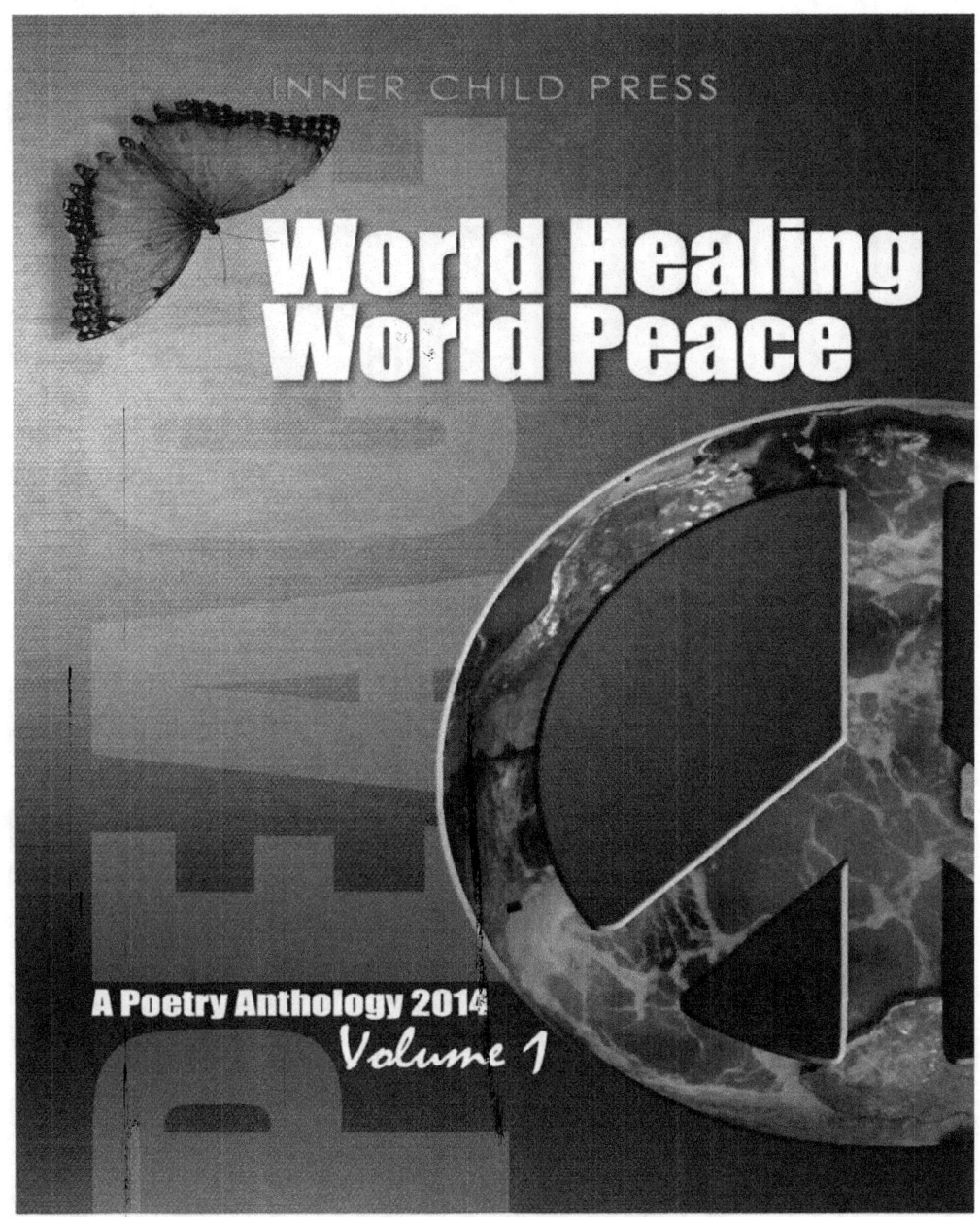

Now Available at

www.innerchildpress.com

Inner Child Press Anthologies

Now Available at

www.innerchildpress.com

Inner Child Press Anthologies

Now Available at

www.innerchildpress.com

Inner Child Press Anthologies

A POETRY ANTHOLOGY
Volume 2

Now Available at
www.innerchildpress.com

Inner Child Press Anthologies

Now Available at

www.innerchildpress.com

Inner Child Press Anthologies

Now Available at

www.innerchildpress.com

Inner Child Press Anthologies

Mandela

The Man

His Life

Its Meaning

Our Words

Poetry ... Commentary & Stories
The Anthological Writers

Now Available at
www.innerchildpress.com

A GATHERING OF WORDS

POETRY FOR
TRAYVON MARTIN

Now Available at
www.innerchildpress.com

Inner Child Press Anthologies

Now Available at

www.innerchildpress.com

Inner Child Press Anthologies

i want my PoEtRy to ...
a collection of the Voices of Many inspired by ...
Monte Smith

i want my PoEtRy to ... volume II
a collection of the Voices of Many inspired by ...
Monte Smith

i want my Poetry to ... volume 3
a collection of the Voices of Many inspired by ...
Monte Smith

I want my poetry to ... volume 4
the conscious poets
inspired by ... Monte Smith

Now Available at
www.innerchildpress.com

Inner Child Press Anthologies

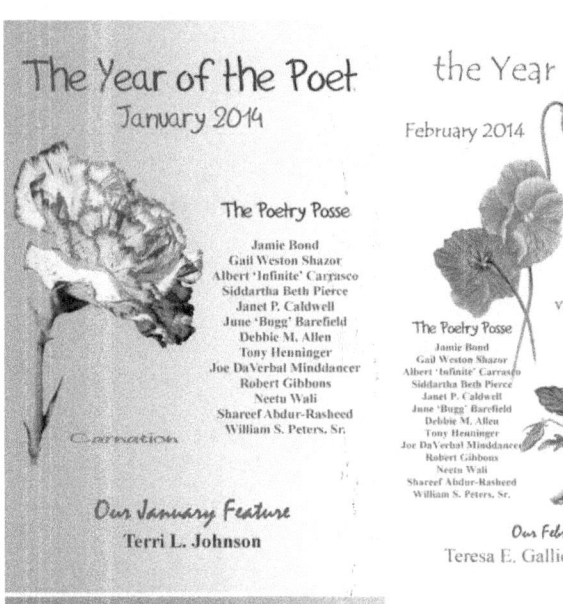

Now Available at

www.innerchildpress.com

Inner Child Press Anthologies

Now Available at

www.innerchildpress.com

Inner Child Press Anthologies

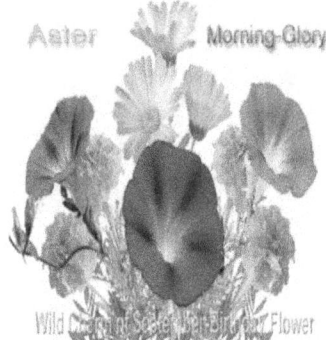

Now Available at

www.innerchildpress.com

Inner Child Press Anthologies

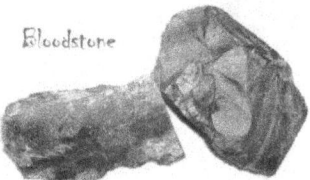

Now Available at

www.innerchildpress.com

Inner Child Press Anthologies

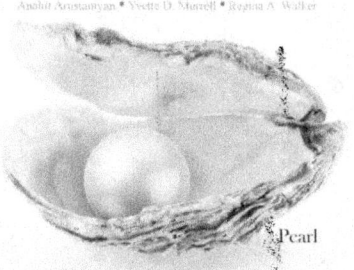

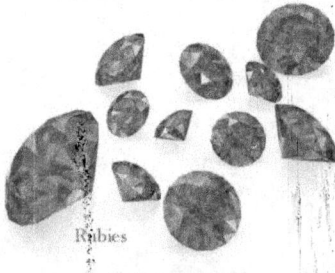

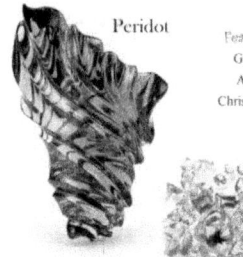

Now Available at

www.innerchildpress.com

Inner Child Press Anthologies

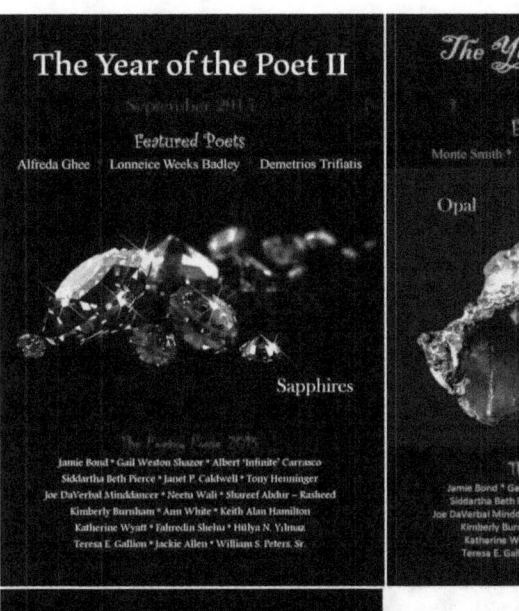

Now Available at

www.innerchildpress.com

Inner Child Press Anthologies

Now Available at

www.innerchildpress.com

Inner Child Press Anthologies

Now Available at

www.innerchildpress.com

Inner Child Press Anthologies

Now Available at

www.innerchildpress.com

Inner Child Press Anthologies

Now Available at

www.innerchildpress.com

Inner Child Press Anthologies

Now Available at

www.innerchildpress.com

Inner Child Press Anthologies

The Year of the Poet IV
September 2017

Featured Poets
Martina Reisz Newberry
Ameer Nassir
Christine Fulco Neal
Robert Neal

The Elm Tree

The Poetry Posse 2017

Gail Weston Shazor * Caroline Nazareno * Bismay Mohanty
Teresa E. Gallion * Anna Jakubczak Vel Ratty Adalan
Joe DaVerbal Minddancer * Shareef Abdur – Rasheed
Albert Carrasco * Kimberly Burnham * Elizabeth Castillo
Hülya N. Yılmaz * Faleeha Hassan * Jackie Davis Allen
Jen Walls * Nizar Sartawi * William S. Peters, Sr.

The Year of the Poet IV
October 2017

Featured Poets
Ahmed Abu Saleem
Nedal Al-Qaeim
Sadeddin Shahin

The Black Walnut Tree

The Poetry Posse 2017

Gail Weston Shazor * Caroline Nazareno * Bismay Mohanty
Teresa E. Gallion * Anna Jakubczak Vel Ratty Adalan
Joe DaVerbal Minddancer * Shareef Abdur – Rasheed
Albert Carrasco * Kimberly Burnham * Elizabeth Castillo
Hülya N. Yılmaz * Faleeha Hassan * Jackie Davis Allen
Jen Walls * Nizar Sartawi * William S. Peters, Sr.

The Year of the Poet IV
November 2017

Featured Poets
Kay Peters
Alfreda D. Ghee
Gabriella Garofalo
Rosemary Cappello

The Tree of Life

The Poetry Posse 2017

Gail Weston Shazor * Caroline Nazareno * Bismay Mohanty
Teresa E. Gallion * Anna Jakubczak Vel Ratty Adalan
Joe DaVerbal Minddancer * Shareef Abdur – Rasheed
Albert Carrasco * Kimberly Burnham * Elizabeth Castillo
Hülya N. Yılmaz * Faleeha Hassan * Jackie Davis Allen
Jen Walls * Nizar Sartawi * William S. Peters, Sr.

The Year of the Poet IV
December 2017

Featured Poets
Justice Clarke
Mariel M. Pabroa
Kiley Brown

The Fig Tree

The Poetry Posse 2017

Gail Weston Shazor * Caroline Nazareno * Bismay Mohanty
Teresa E. Gallion * Anna Jakubczak Vel Ratty Adalan
Joe DaVerbal Minddancer * Shareef Abdur – Rasheed
Albert Carrasco * Kimberly Burnham * Elizabeth Castillo
Hülya N. Yılmaz * Faleeha Hassan * Jackie Davis Allen
Jen Walls * Nizar Sartawi * William S. Peters, Sr.

Now Available at
www.innerchildpress.com

Inner Child Press Anthologies

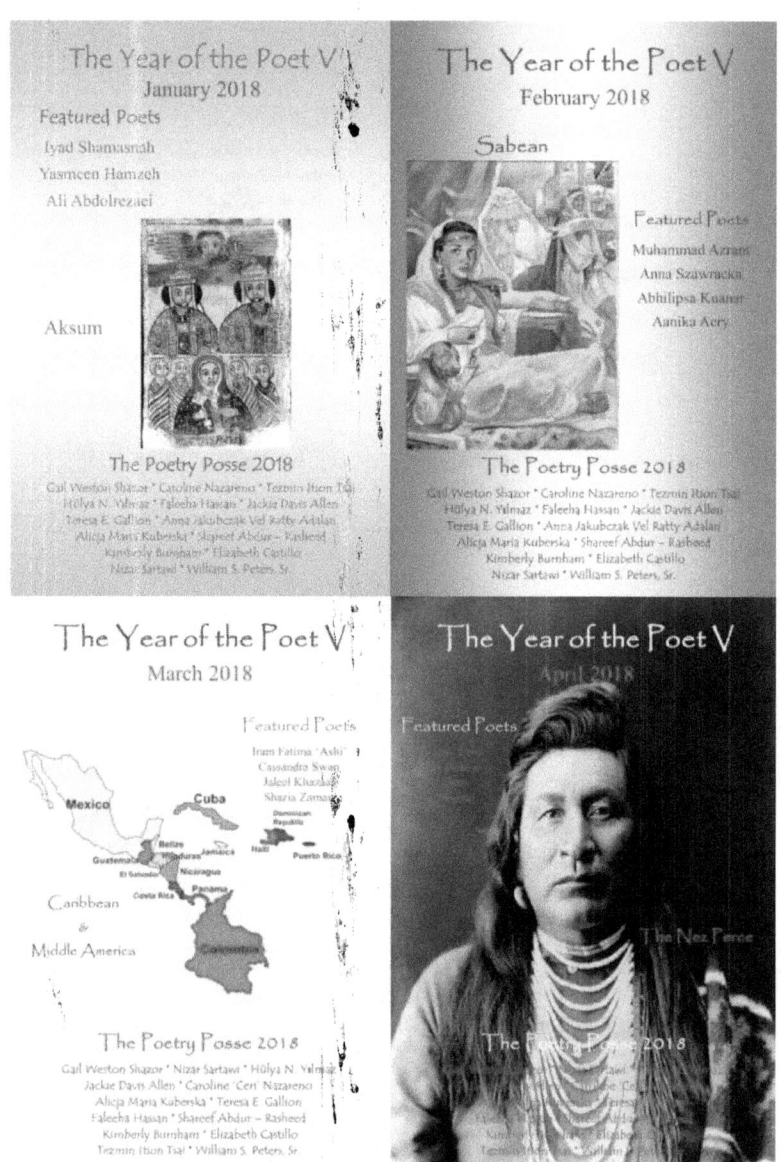

Now Available at

www.innerchildpress.com

Inner Child Press Anthologies

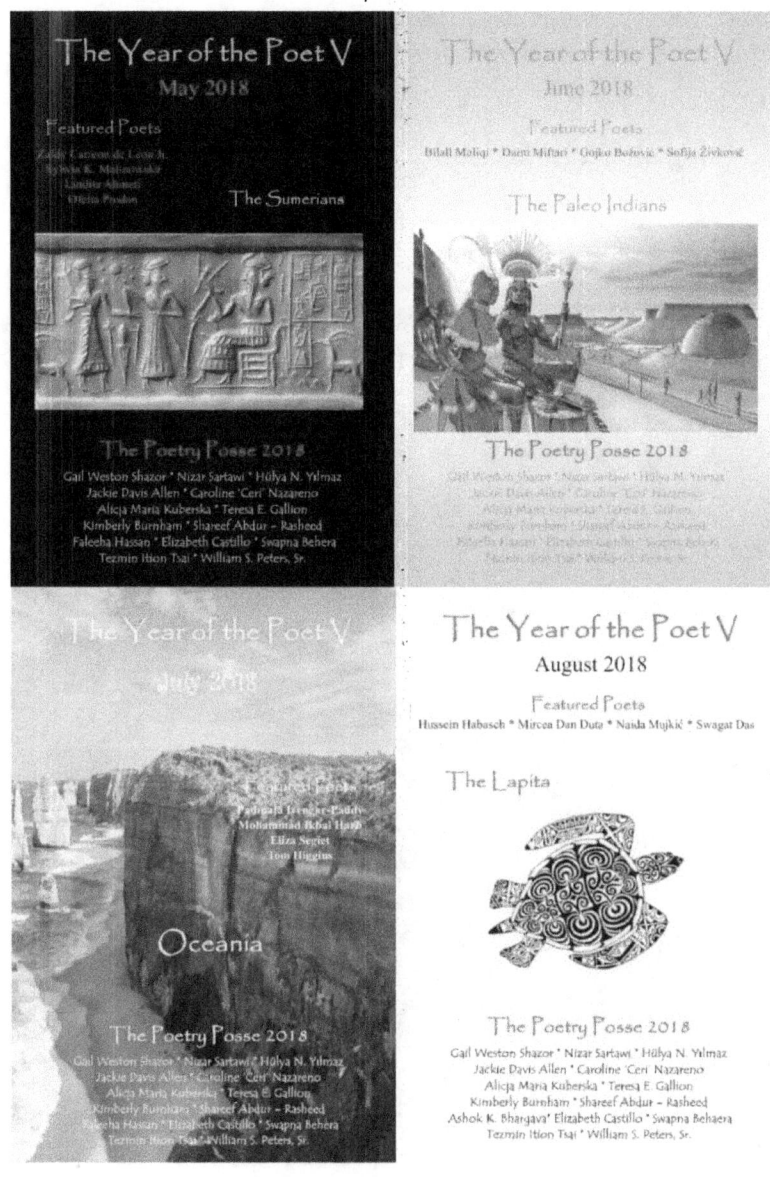

Now Available at

www.innerchildpress.com

Inner Child Press Anthologies

Now Available at
www.innerchildpress.com

Inner Child Press Anthologies

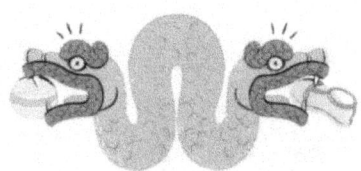

Now Available at

www.innerchildpress.com

Inner Child Press Anthologies

Now Available at

www.innerchildpress.com

Inner Child Press Anthologies

Now Available at

www.innerchildpress.com

Inner Child Press Anthologies

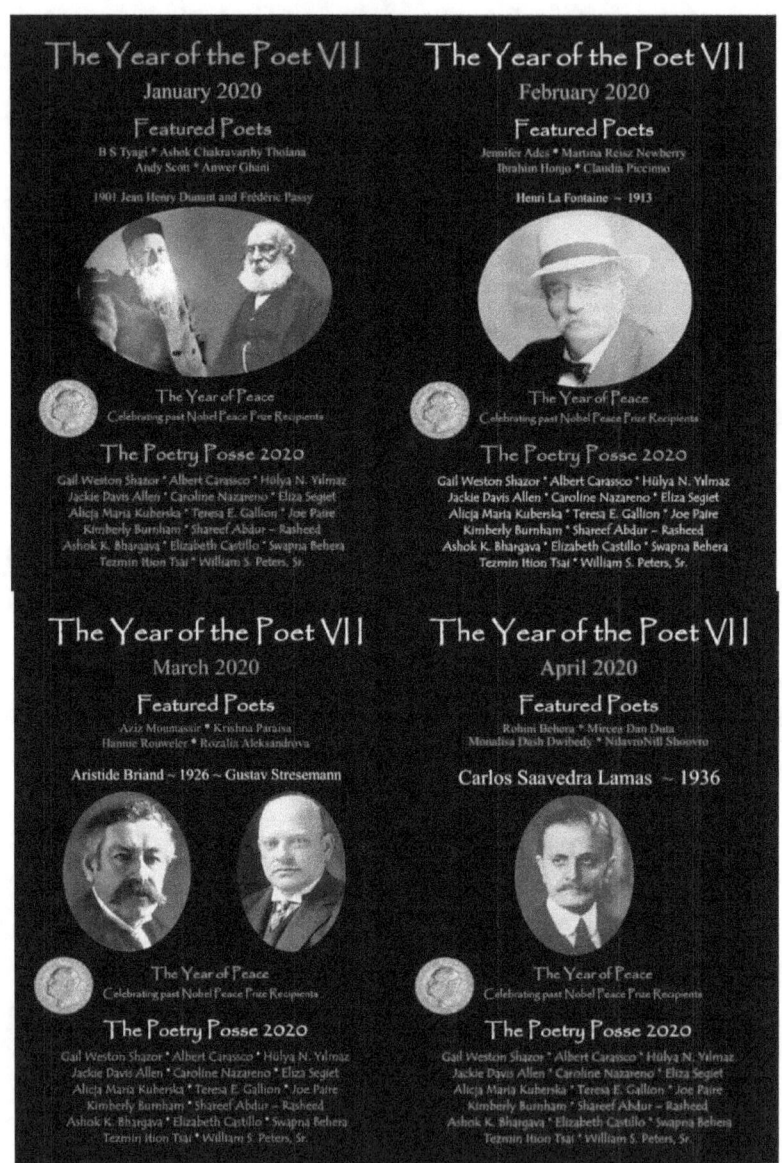

Now Available at

www.innerchildpress.com

Inner Child Press Anthologies

Now Available at

www.innerchildpress.com

Inner Child Press Anthologies

Now Available at

www.innerchildpress.com

and there is much, much more !

visit . . .

www.innerchildpress.com/anthologies-sales-special.php

Also check out our Authors and all the wonderful Books Available at :

www.innerchildpress.com/authors-pages

www.worldhealingworldpeacepoetry.com

Inner Child Press International

Inner Child Press International is a publishing company founded and operated by writers. Our personal publishing experiences provide us an intimate understanding of the sometimes-daunting challenges writers, new and seasoned, may face in the business of publishing and marketing their creative "Written Work".

For more Information:

Inner Child Press International

www.innerchildpress.com
intouch@innerchildpress.com

'building bridges of cultural understanding'

www.innerchildpress.com